A-LEVEL YEAR 2
STUDENT GUIDE

EDEXCEL

Psychology

Psychological skills

Christine Brain

PHILIP ALLAN FOR
HODDER
EDUCATION
AN HACHETTE UK COMPANY

Philip Allan, an imprint of Hodder Education, an Hachette UK company, Blenheim Court, George Street, Banbury, Oxfordshire OX16 5BH

Orders

Bookpoint Ltd, 130 Park Drive, Milton Park, Abingdon, Oxfordshire OX14 4SB

tel: 01235 827827

fax: 01235 400401

e-mail: education@bookpoint.co.uk

Lines are open 9.00 a.m.–5.00 p.m., Monday to Saturday, with a 24-hour message answering service. You can also order through the Hodder Education website: www.hoddereducation.co.uk

© Christine Brain 2016

ISBN 978-1-4718-5943-4

First printed 2016

Impression number 5 4 3 2 1

Year 2020 2019 2018 2017 2016

This Guide has been written specifically to support students preparing for the Edexcel A-level Psychology examinations. The content has been neither approved nor endorsed by Edexcel and remains the sole responsibility of the author.

Typeset by Integra Software Services Pvt. Ltd., Pondicherry, India

Cover photograph: agsandrew/Fotolia

Printed in Italy

Hachette UK's policy is to use papers that are natural, renewable and recyclable products and made from wood grown in sustainable forests. The logging and manufacturing processes are expected to conform to the environmental regulations of the country of origin.

Contents

Content Guidance

Questions & Answers

■ Getting the most from this book

Exam tips
Advice on key points in the text to help you learn and recall content, avoid pitfalls, and polish your exam technique in order to boost your grade.

Knowledge check
Rapid-fire questions throughout the Content Guidance section to check your understanding.

Knowledge check answers
1 Turn to the back of the book for the Knowledge check answers.

Summaries
■ Each core topic is rounded off by a bullet-list summary for quick-check reference of what you need to know.

Exam-style questions

Commentary on the questions

Tips on what you need to do to gain full marks, indicated by the icon **e**

Sample student answers

Practise the questions, then look at the student answers that follow.

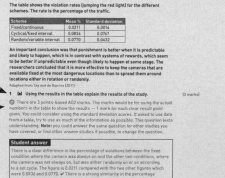

Commentary on sample student answers

Find out how many marks each answer would be awarded in the exam and then read the comments (preceded by the icon **e**) following each student answer.

■ About this book

This guide covers the synoptic topic of the Edexcel GCE A-level Psychology specification. This is Topic 9 and it is assessed by Paper 3.

Table 1 shows the overall A-level qualification. A-level Paper 1 examines the four topics from Year 1 with the addition of issues and debates. A-level Paper 2 covers applications of psychology with the addition of issues and debates. A-level Paper 3 covers psychological skills, including specifically the method, studies and issues and debates from the A-level course.

- Student Guide 1 covers the first two topic areas in Year 1 of the A-level (social and cognitive psychology).
- Student Guide 2 covers the last two topic areas in Year 1 of the A-level (biological psychology and learning theories).
- Student Guide 3 covers Topics 5 to 8 (clinical, criminological, child and health psychology), which are examined in A-level Paper 2.
- Student Guide 4 covers Topic 9 (method, studies and issues and debates), which is examined in A-level Paper 3.

Table 1 Overview of A level Papers (**bold** indicates covered in this guide)

A-level Year 1	A-level Year 2
Paper 1: social, cognitive, biological, learning (including issues and debates)	Paper 2: clinical and one from criminological, child and health (including issues and debates)
Paper 3: psychological skills (method, studies, issues and debates) Paper 3 is a 'revision' paper because the material has already been covered throughout the course and it is a synoptic paper because you can be asked to draw on your learning across the course.	

Aims

This guide is not a textbook — there is no substitute for reading the required material and taking notes. Nor does it tell you the actual questions on your paper. The aim of this guide is to provide you with a clear understanding of the requirements of A-level Paper 3, and to advise you on how best to meet these requirements. This guide will also help to an extent with Papers 1 and 2 because it covers Topic 9, which is a revision topic, drawing your learning together. This guide looks at:

- the psychology you need to know about
- what you need to be able to do and what skills you need
- how you could go about learning the necessary material
- what is being examined, including mathematical skills
- what you should expect in the examination
- how you could tackle the different styles of exam question
- the format of the exam, including what questions might look like
- how questions might be marked, including examples of answers, with examiner's comments

How to use this guide

A good way of using this guide is to read it through in the order in which it is presented. Alternatively, you can consider each topic in the Content Guidance section, and then turn to a relevant question in the Questions & Answers section. Whichever way you use the guide, try some of the questions yourself to test your learning.

Questions & Answers

Note that cross-references in the Content Guidance are given to answers in the Questions & Answers section that provide more information on particular areas of content.

Glossary

A list of terms is included at the end of this guide (pages 78–83). They are organised alphabetically and subdivided into the three sections —methods, review of studies, and issues and debates. This list of definitions can help you in your revision.

Content Guidance

■ Section A: Methods

This section reviews the methods material you have covered throughout your course. **Methodology** includes everything to do with methods in a study. It covers some main research methods from your course, including questionnaire and interview to gather self-report data, experiment, observation and correlation, and issues related to these research methods. There is emphasis on different types of data as well as issues like sampling. There is a section on other research methods too, such as twin and adoption studies, and longitudinal versus cross-sectional designs.

Analysis of data is focused on both quantitative and qualitative data, as well as issues around writing up a psychology report and the all-important issue of ethics, regarding using both humans and animals.

Types of data

Primary and secondary data

Primary data

Primary data are data that researchers collect themselves, first hand.

■ An example of gathering primary data is Milgram (1963) who ran an experiment collecting data from **participants**.

Secondary data

Secondary data are **data** that are already collected by researchers and then used for a new purpose by different researchers.

■ A **meta-analysis** (page 23) uses secondary data when drawing together studies focusing on a similar research question.

> **Exam tip**
>
> For terms and methodology ideas be ready to offer strengths and weaknesses, advantages or disadvantages. Prepare a table showing the advantages and disadvantages of using primary or secondary data. You studied these types of data in clinical psychology. Check your notes for the information you need.

> **Exam tip**
>
> List all the terms used in this section (see Summary on page 32), and make sure you can define them. This will help you to feel in control of the Methods part of Paper 3 and will also help with revision of methodology for Papers 1 and 2.

> **Exam tip**
>
> When revising terms like primary and secondary data make sure you can define the term and give an example to show your understanding. Work on around 3 marks being required — so you need to say enough for 3 marks.

	Statement about a study	Gathers primary or secondary data
a	Researchers tallied how aggressive children were depending on which type of video game they played	
b	A meta-analysis drew together data from eight studies about the effectiveness of drug therapy to treat heroin	
c	Researchers compared numbers of people with schizophrenia focusing on age and gender using government statistics for each year over 10 years	

Qualitative and quantitative data

Qualitative data are words, pictures, photographs or songs — where data are 'quality' rather than numbers. **Quantitative data** are numbers, such as percentages or ratings from self-report data.

Table 1 Strengths and weaknesses of quantitative data

Strengths	Weaknesses
Use measures that can be analysed statistically to give strength to conclusions	Often forced choice answers so can lack validity
Use measures that can be repeated and compared, so reliability can be checked	Measuring instruments cannot be changed once the study has started so there is inflexibility

Table 2 Strengths and weaknesses of qualitative data

Strengths	Weaknesses
Data use the participants' own meanings	Hard to generalise to other people and other situations
Useful when the issue in question is complex as complexity can be focused on	Data analysis can be time-consuming, such as thematic analysis, which has a number of steps

Questions & Answers

Methods Qualitative data Q1b refers to the advantages of qualitative data over quantitative data, including an example from an unseen study.

Questions & Answers

Research methods Qualitative data Q1a refers to the advantages of using qualitative data from different research methods.

Knowledge check 1

Copy and complete this table to show understanding of the difference between primary and secondary data.

Exam tip

The distinction between these two types of data is useful for evaluating a study. In general, qualitative data will have a **validity** that quantitative do not, and quantitative will show **replicability** and **reliability** that qualitative data will not.

Knowledge check 2

From your course give two studies that gather qualitative data and two that use quantitative data.

Sampling techniques

There are four **sampling** techniques you need to know about in your course. These are random, stratified, volunteer and opportunity sampling. The aim of sampling is to get a **representative sample**, which means the people in the study represent the population of interest.

Random sampling

Random sampling means that everyone in the chosen population has an equal chance of being in the sample. One way to do this is to put all the names in a box and pull one out at a time until reaching the required number. Each time a name is pulled out, all the names have an equal chance of being chosen.

Random sampling is best when it comes to **generalising** as people are randomly allocated (**randomising** is used) into **conditions** so there is not likely to be bias. One problem is that it is often not possible to have a complete list of everyone in the target population.

Stratified sampling

Stratified sampling is used when the researchers need to be sure there are participants in each of the categories of interest so they make sure they have people in each 'strata'. The numbers in each category should match the proportions in the population. For example, researchers might target females aged '20 to 39', '40 to 59', and '60 and over', and then males in the same three age groups.

Stratified sampling is efficient when it comes to making sure the sample meets requirements though there can be bias because once the quota is reached nobody else can be involved, which means some are excluded.

Volunteer sampling

Volunteer sampling is when all participants have put themselves forward, such as when Milgram (1963) advertised for people to be participants.

One strength of this is that volunteer sampling might be less time-consuming than, say, stratified sampling. However, a problem is bias. People who volunteer might not be the same as people who do not, and only those seeing the advert (for example) could take part.

Opportunity sampling

Opportunity sampling is based on convenience and people from the target population used are those available at the time (and willing to take part). Students coming out of the library, if used as participants, are an opportunity sample.

Using opportunity sampling is efficient in terms of time and can be ethical as participants know they are taking part in a study. However, it is likely that a sample taken at one moment in time in one place has bias as not everyone in the target population can be in the sample.

Exam tip

In social psychology you covered the four sampling techniques including their strengths and weaknesses so use that material when revising. If you chose criminological psychology you looked at sampling there too. Look for studies you have covered that use these types of sampling to add evidence to your answers.

Knowledge check 3

(a) Which sampling technique did Milgram (1963) use? (b) Which sampling technique did Watson and Rayner (1920) use?

Exam tip

In the brief descriptions of the four types of sampling given here there are some comments about their relative strengths and weaknesses. Draw up a table and complete it to show strengths and weaknesses of each of the four sampling techniques.

Experimental/research designs

There are three ways that participants can be organised in research. They are either put into independent groups, into a repeated measures design or a matched pairs design is used.

Independent groups design

In an **independent groups design** there are different participants for each condition. This means that in the different conditions participants do not get tired as they are just doing one condition, and they are not likely to get bored because of doing more than one of the conditions, so an advantage is there are no order effects. However, **participant variables** might give the results bias. Different participants in different conditions might mean differences in individuals might affect the results. For example, in one condition participants might have different relevant skills than in another condition. Random allocation to groups can help to avoid participant variables.

- Sebastián and Hernández-Gill (2012) used an independent groups design when they compared digit span in those in different age groups as people can only be in one age group.
- Sherif et al. (1954/1961) used independent groups in that the boys were either in the Eagles group or the Rattlers group, though there was some matching so to an extent their study can be seen as matched pairs.

Exam tip

It can sometimes be good not to be too specific. For example, you can say Sherif et al. (1954/1961) used independent groups, justifying the claim, but you can then present an argument that there is matching. It is the discussion that has value and shows knowledge and understanding.

Repeated measures design

In a **repeated measures** design the same participants are in all the conditions in a study. A difficulty is that one person doing all the conditions might get tired after the first one, which is the **fatigue effect**. Another person might get better after the first condition, which is the **practice effect**. These are also **order effects**. One way around order effects is to use **counterbalancing**, which means there is alternation with regard to which condition is done first. **Randomisation** is also useful, when the condition each person does first is decided randomly.

- Baddeley (1966b) used a repeated measures design when he compared scores for the same person after a gap with those before a gap. However, he used an independent groups design too when looking at scores of those with 'sound alike' words with those with a control list.

Matched pairs design

A third research design is when different participants do the different conditions but the participants are matched on important **variables** such as age, gender or something suiting the study, such as driving ability. If a study is called 'matched pairs' then it is treated as repeated measures for test purposes because it is 'as if' the participants are the same — they are matched. A **matched pairs** design helps with participant variables (because of the matching), and avoids order effects (participants are different people), however, there can still be participant variables (participants are still different people).

- Bandura, Ross and Ross (1961) can call their study a matched pairs design because they matched the children regarding their aggression.

Questions & Answers

Methods Unseen study: an animal laboratory experiment Q1b refers to how the unseen study has both a repeated measures and an independent groups element.

Table 3 Strengths and weaknesses of the different experimental/research designs

Type of sampling	Strengths	Weaknesses
Independent groups	No order effects, such as a fatigue or a practice effect and easier to administer in some ways because it does not take as long for each participant	The study needs more participants, which can affect ethics in that if there is some deceit, more are deceived. There may be differences between the individuals in each condition, giving bias in the results
Repeated measures	Participant variables are less of a problem as the same person does all the conditions. Fewer participants are needed so the study can be run more quickly and there might be ethical gains in using fewer participants	There can be order effects which affect the results. The participants might show demand characteristics, meaning they guess what the study is about and react accordingly
Matched pairs	Helps to control for individual differences so that participant variables do not affect the results. There will not be order effects as there are in a repeated measures design	Even though it helps with individual differences, the participants are still different and such differences might affect the results. The researcher(s) might not match all the required variables

Exam tip

You can learn brief strengths and weaknesses, such as of a research design or sampling technique. For example, you can learn that repeated measures designs can be subject to order effects. However, make sure you can explain your answer to show understanding.

Exam tip

When an experimental or research design is talked about, it will be about the way participants are allocated to groups in a study. However, 'design' can also mean how the study is set up, so watch for the different uses of the term 'design'.

Knowledge check 4

If researchers wanted to look at memory for a list of words to see if using categories when learning the words helped compared with having the words randomly presented in the list, they could use any of the three designs. Explain how each of the designs could be used.

Hypotheses

There are three types of **hypothesis** you need to know about: the null hypothesis, the alternate, and a form of the alternate, which is known as the experimental hypothesis.

In all types of hypothesis the independent variable(s) and the dependent variable(s) must be **operationalised**, which means saying exactly what is varied (the IV) and what is measured (the DV).

The null hypothesis

The **null hypothesis** is the statement that what is expected by the researcher(s) is not going to happen. The researcher(s) make a statement about what they expect and then the null hypothesis is that any difference or relationship they expect to find is not going to occur in a statistically significant way, and any different there is must be due to chance or to something else that is unexpected.

The idea is that the null hypothesis is tested as if it is true (that there is no difference or relationship) and it is rejected if there is enough significance to show that the results are not likely to be due to chance.

- Raine et al.'s (1997) idea that those pleading not guilty to murder by reason of insanity will have differences in certain brain regions compared with a control group would have a null hypothesis something like 'people pleading not guilty to murder by reason of insanity will not show differences in brain regions compared with a control group'.

The alternate/alternative hypothesis

The **alternate/alternative hypothesis** is the statement the researcher(s) make about what they expect to find. The alternate is the opposite to the null hypothesis. If when the null hypothesis is tested it is found that there is a level of significance showing the results are not likely to be due to chance at the chosen level (such as $p<.01$) then the alternate hypothesis is accepted and the null is rejected.

- If a researcher wants to see whether presenting participants with a list separated into categories (e.g. 'colours' and 'places people live') gives better recall than if the participants are given a list of the same words but in random order, the hypothesis is 'there is a difference in that participants seeing a list of 20 words separated into categories recall more words from the list (in any order) than participants seeing a list of the same 20 words but in random order'.

Knowledge check 5

In the example given about a study using a list of 20 words presented in categories or randomly, which is the IV, and how is it operationalised, and which is the DV, and how is it operationalised?

Exam tip

If you are asked to write out any hypothesis in an exam, check after doing so that both the IV and the DV are fully operationalised, which means fully made measurable. For example, not just 'recall' for the DV.

The experimental hypothesis

The **experimental hypothesis** is the alternate hypothesis when the study uses the experimental method. The example given above about recall of categorised words compared with words presented randomly is an experimental hypothesis.

Table 4 Examples of the different types of hypothesis

Type of hypothesis	Example
Experimental hypothesis	Children aged 5 to 6 years have a shorter digit span than young people aged 17 years
Alternate hypothesis (when the method is not experiment)	The more people self-report authoritarian beliefs, such as their belief that society should have strong rules, the higher their prejudice score, such as believing crime relates to race
Null hypothesis	There is no difference in digit span between children aged 5 to 6 years and young people aged 17 years

Directional and non-directional: features of hypotheses

An alternate/experimental hypothesis can be directional or non-directional. A **directional** hypothesis is where researchers predict direction in the results, such as saying recall of words is better in a certain condition than in another (directional). When they do not know which condition would be better, this is **non-directional** and results can go either way.

Table 5 Examples of directional and non-directional hypotheses

Example	Directional or non-directional hypothesis
Children aged 5 to 6 years have a shorter digit span than young people aged 17 years	Directional (says 'shorter')
The more people self-report authoritarian beliefs, such as their belief that society should have strong rules, the higher their prejudice score, such as believing crime relates to race	Directional (says 'the more...the higher...')
There is a difference in recall of 10 words from a list depending on whether the list involves words that all sound alike or whether the list has words of a similar length but the words do not sound alike	Non-directional (does not say which list would be better recalled)

Questionnaires and interviews

Research methods that survey people to get their ideas and opinions include questionnaires and interviews. You need to know some features of each.

Self-report data

Questions & Answers

Methods Unseen study: a questionnaire Q1c refers to issues with self-report data such as social desirability, which causes bias.

Exam tip

When you are answering a question about significance of results add a comment about either rejecting the null hypothesis or accepting the alternate/experimental hypothesis, as is mentioned later (page 26) when discussing levels of significance.

Exam tip

In the method part of psychological skills there are a lot of terms. You could use index cards with a term on one side and an explanation on the other to help your learning. Draw up these cards using the glossary.

Exam tip

To help with using inferential tests, link directional and non-directional with one-tailed (when the hypothesis is directional) and two-tailed (when direction is not predicted) when it comes to statistical testing (page 26).

Self-report data are gathered using interviewing or questionnaires, and refer to data a person has given about themselves. There is a possibility that validity is lacking, such as when someone does not tell the truth, for example, they may say what they think is appropriate (**social desirability**). There is also the claim that self-report data are valid data because they come directly from the individual with little interpretation by a researcher. **Self-rating** involves giving a rating score about oneself such as rating our own level of prejudice.

- Cohrs et al. (2012) gathered self-report data as well as peer-report data and compared the two, finding that self-report data are reliable (the peer-report data matched them).

Questionnaires

Questionnaires can use open and closed questions. Closed questions can use ranked scales.

- Cohrs et al. (2012) used questionnaires to gather data, using ranking of items.

Standardised instructions are used in questionnaires so that all **respondents** are given the same detail before they start — this can include both practical instructions and ethics too. A **pilot study** is often carried out to check items and questions, to make sure they are clearly understood in the same way by all respondents. **Personal data** are gathered, such as gender, age, occupation, education level and social group, depending on the study's requirements.

Open questions

Open questions gather data about attitudes and opinions and let respondents give data more freely than if closed questions are used. Qualitative data are gathered.

Closed questions

Closed questions are when options are restricted, such as giving the option of 'yes' or 'no' or a choice of age groups to choose from. Closed questions gather quantitative data (e.g. how many respondents answer 'yes' and how many say 'no').

Ranked-scale questions

Ranked scales/ranked data are gathered when closed questions ask respondents to rank their replies. One way of doing this is to use a **Likert-type** scale, which is where respondents can choose from 'Strongly agree' to 'Strongly disagree' or something similar. Often a 7-point scale is used.

Questions & Answers

Methods Unseen study: a questionnaire Q1b refers to Likert-ranked data.

Response set

A **response set** is when someone starts answering in one way and then goes on in the same way, such as starting responding agreeing to being prejudiced and continuing with 'agree' throughout. Statements should be changed so that 'agree' is the response to 'not prejudiced' sometimes as well.

Exam tip

You may not have covered Cohrs et al., and there may be other examples in this book you have not covered. In such cases find an example you can use as that can help to show understanding of the method issues you need to know about.

Exam tip

You can be asked to write a suitable closed or open question in a given scenario. It is useful to give an example that requires a question mark. Otherwise be sure for closed questions that you give the choice (e.g. yes/no) so that you present the item as a question.

Knowledge check 6

Imagine a study asking for self-report data about prejudiced attitudes. Write one closed question and one open question that might be found on a questionnaire.

Table 6 Strengths and weaknesses of questionnaires as a method

Strengths	Weaknesses
Can gather both qualitative and quantitative data with the benefits of each, such as depth and detail as well as comparable data more easily analysed than qualitative data	Can lack validity in that there can be social desirability, meaning someone says what they think they ought to say
They can be practical in collecting a large amount of data in a reasonably cost effective way and involving a large sample	There can be interpretation of the items on a questionnaire, so data might not be as comparable as might be assumed
	There might be a **researcher effect** in that someone's answers are affected by the characteristics of the researcher such as their age, appearance or gender (females might respond differently to a male or a female researcher)

Interviews

Interviews can be structured, unstructured or semi-structured and tend to gather self-report data. Qualitative data are gathered though there can be some quantitative data. There should be validity though social desirability as well as **subjectivity** in analysing the data can all bring bias.

■ Vallentine et al. (2010) used interviewing in their study looking at the value of giving offender patients information about their disorder.

Structured interviews

Structured interviews involve the interviewer asking each **interviewee** the same set of questions, which are limited and are prepared before the interview. There is not much opportunity for a respondent to expand on their answers though there can be some open questions. There is **standardisation** in the wording of questions/items and the interviewer remains neutral.

Unstructured interviews

In an **unstructured interview** the interviewer sets a time for an interview and has a focus for the interview which the interviewee understands. However, unlike a structured interview, the interviewer builds rapport with the respondents, aiming to get them to express themselves and choose what they contribute as data.

Semi-structured interviews

A **semi-structured interview** is formal and there is a **schedule** with more detail than in an unstructured interview, giving a list of questions and topics to be covered. However, the list does not involve set questions as in a structured interview. Also the interviewer can move away from the questions as they see fit, even though they would then come back to the list and carry on, using the structure.

> **Exam tip**
>
> If asked about interviewing as a research method you can explain all three types of interview to add detail to your answer. Giving some examples of studies using interviews would help to show understanding if you explain how interviewing is used in the example.

Knowledge check 7

Why would bias from social desirability reflect lack of validity in an answer?

> **Exam tip**
>
> You can be asked for strengths or weaknesses of a research method (or issue), and you can be asked about advantages and disadvantages. You can also be asked to 'evaluate' in general. You can use the same ideas to answer such questions, but you should tailor your answer to the specific question.

> **Exam tip**
>
> If giving a strength or weakness that is about a comparison, such as 'more easily analysed' be sure to add 'than...'. A comparison should be fully explained.

Table 7 Strengths and weaknesses of interviews as a method

Type of interview	Strengths	Weaknesses
Structured	Less training for interviewers as the questions/items are set so can be efficient and cheaper than using trained interviewers. Comparisons can be made between responses of different people	There is little opportunity for expanding on answers so they can be restricting and perhaps less valid than less structured interviewing. They can be time-consuming such as when compared with postal questionnaires
Unstructured	They are good when not much is known about an area of study as they give a lot of rich and detailed valid data about such an area, from which more research ideas can develop	It is not as easy to compare data from different respondents as in a structured interview because the respondent leads the interview and may go down a unique route. Data are not as generalisable
Semi-structured	Questions are done beforehand which helps the interviewer to keep on track and can help to make comparisons between responses of different participants. There is still the opportunity for respondents to expand on their answers, unlike structured interviewing, and this can add validity to the data	Interviews can take a long time which means it is likely fewer participants can be involved than in a quicker structured interview or questionnaire. There might be a lack of **generalisability** if the sample size is small and the sample limited

Experiments

Experiments are used in psychology to look for differences in how variables affect one another. They are used to look for cause-and-effect conclusions. They have specific features.

Table 8 Features of experiments as a research method

Features of the experimental research method
A research question gives a specific focus arising from theory and variables are operationalised, one being the independent variable (IV) — such as the meaning of words manipulated to look at recall. For example, a list of 10 words of similar meaning compared with a list of 10 words matched but without the same meaning. It is the **independent variable** that is manipulated.
The result of manipulating the independent variable is the **dependent variable (DV)** which is measured. An example might be recall of 10 words in the order they were presented in (depending on whether they have the same meaning or are matched words but not with the same meaning).
Apart from the IV and the DV all other variables (called **extraneous variables**) must be controlled including participant variables and **situational variables**. These might be gender or age (participant) or noise in the environment (situational).
If extraneous variables are controlled for, there are no **confounding variables** and cause-and-effect conclusions are drawn.
The experimental hypothesis is accepted if the results are statistically significant (see later when looking at levels of significance, page 26) and the theory supported and/or more testing is done.

Independent and dependent variables

In an experiment a main variable is the independent variable, which is what is varied to see its effect. The various **conditions** of the experiment are the independent variable and what is measured as a result of these conditions is the dependent variable. For example, it might be thought that age affects driving ability. Age could

Knowledge check 8

Which type of interview of the three explained would you expect to get more valid data? Give reasons for your answer.

Exam tip

The example used in Table 8 is part of Baddeley (1966b). You can use the studies you have covered as examples when explaining issues about research methods.

Knowledge check 9

When is a variable called a 'confounding variable'?

be 18 to 25 year olds as the young group, 26 to 40 year olds as the middle group, and 50+ as the older age group. Participants all drive round a track laid out by using traffic cones, using the same car. The number of cones they knock over is counted. The three conditions of the independent variable are the three age groups. The dependent variable is how many cones are knocked over.

Table 9 Examples of independent and dependent variables

Example	Independent variable	Dependent variable
Someone in the street asking for directions wearing a hat is less likely to be identified in a photo lineup that includes their photo than someone not wearing a hat	Whether the person asking for directions is wearing a hat or not	Whether the person is picked out in a photo lineup that their photo is in
Boys are more likely to reward by giving more counters to someone from their own group than someone they see as an out-group member	Whether the person being rewarded is represented as being in the boys' in-group or their out-group	How many counters the boys give

Questions & Answers

Methods Unseen study: an animal laboratory experiment Q1a refers to the different conditions in an experiment.

Additional features of experiments

There can be **experimenter effects**, which means data are affected by issues connected with the experimenter, such as their dress, their manner, their gender or their age.

Experiments can have an **experimental group** and a **control group**, with the experimental group having the 'treatment' and the control group being there to give a **baseline measure**, to show what would happen without the 'treatment' as a comparison.

Randomised controlled trials (RCTs) are where one group is involved in a treatment (the **treatment group**) (e.g. CBT for phobias) and one is on a waiting list (the control group) for the treatment. The important part is to randomise which group a participant is in, to make the comparison fair.

A **placebo** is when a 'dummy' treatment is used so that participants do not know which group they are in, such as one group having a drug therapy and one a 'sugar pill' — which is the placebo.

In experiments a **single-blind technique** can be used to help to avoid bias, where the participants do not know which group they are in. A **double-blind technique** can be used where neither the person running the experiment nor the participant knows which group they are in.

Exam tip

Practise picking out the IV and the DV in the studies you have looked at, such as Baddeley (1966b), Pavlov's 1927 work or Bandura's studies looking at aggression in children. Or you could make up some studies of your own.

Exam tip

There are a lot of terms included here but being able to use these terms should help your revision and your answers. Make lists or diagrams to help you remember the key terms.

Laboratory experiments versus field experiments

A **laboratory experiment** has all the features of an experiment but takes place in an artificial and controlled setting.

Questions & Answers

Methods Unseen study: an animal laboratory experiment Q1c refers to practical issues when using animals in laboratory experiments in psychology to find out about human behaviour.

Field experiments are the same as laboratory experiments in many of their features, but they are in the natural setting and situation. There is no artificial controlled laboratory and so the results show greater validity. This is because they measure what they claim to measure rather than something artificially produced as might be the case in a laboratory experiment. However, less ability to control what is going on around the set up situation means they can lack reliability.

Table 10 Strengths and weaknesses of field and laboratory experiments

Type of experiment	Strengths	Weaknesses
Laboratory	A lot of control means they can be repeated and tested for reliability. Reliability means the results will be found if a study is repeated. The control also means cause and effect conclusions are possible	Having control has strengths, but a weakness is data can lack validity as the setting is artificial (to get the control required). Reducing what is studied to a few conditions means the whole situation and any complexity can be missed
Field	The setting is not controlled which means there is more validity than in a laboratory situation. There are other controls, however, so there can be reliability	The lack of control over the setting can mean lack of reliability. Perhaps less generalisable if in a specific setting

Questions & Answers

Issues and debates Use of psychological knowledge in society Q1 focuses on reducing prejudice as one key question for society. In the answer there is discussion about field experiments versus laboratory experiments, considering issues such as validity and reliability.

Observations

You need to study both structured and naturalistic observations and issues around doing **observations**.

Structured and naturalistic observations

Structured observations

Structured observations are when a situation is set up, to be observed rather than someone observing a natural situation 'in action'. A situation tends to be set up in an artificial environment with standardised procedures. The strange situation procedure, developed by Mary Ainsworth, is an example of a structured observation. Often observation is from behind a screen and done by more than one person to get **inter-observer reliability** or **inter-rater reliability**. Behaviour is often coded and **tallying** is used.

Naturalistic observations

Naturalistic observations take place in the participants' natural environment and behaviour is observed as it occurs, recorded in the best way possible. Play has been studied using naturalistic observation, such as by Sylva and by Melhuish, both looking at early years development.

Types of observation

Participant and non-participant

Participant observation is where the person gathering the data has a role in the situation being observed and is part of it. **Non-participant observation** is where the observer is separate from what is being observed — they are not participating.

Overt and covert

Overt observation is where the participants know about the observation and **covert observation** is where the observation is done secretly — the participants are not aware they are part of an observation.

> **Exam tip**
>
> Experiments can use observation such as looking at what helping behaviour occurs when a room (artificially) fills with smoke. However, when a study is an experiment, carried out in a very controlled way, 'experiment' is the research method.

Table 11 Strengths and weaknesses of structured and naturalistic observations

Type of observation	Strengths	Weaknesses
Structured	Replication is relatively easy, given the standardisation used, so reliability can be tested for. If coding and tallying are used, analysis can use statistics from which firmer conclusions can be drawn than when qualitative data are used	Validity can be a problem because of **demand characteristics** — participants know they are being watched, which can affect their behaviour. Also validity is negatively affected by the structured situation
Naturalistic	Good **ecological validity** because it is the natural situation and setting that is observed. Also useful when carrying out research that is new, so ideas for further study can be generated	Can be hard to generalise as specific and possibly unique situations are studied. There is less reliability because less possibility of replicating that specific situation
Participant	The observer is accepted so does not disrupt the situation and also has insider understanding which can be useful	The observer might not have the opportunity to record what is happening and might not be able to take an unbiased stance, seeing with fresh eyes
Non-participant	The observer has time to observe and record and will not be affected by previous experience	The situation might be different if someone is there observing
Overt	Ethically it is good as participants know they are being observed	There might be an effect on behaviour
Covert	Behaviour is likely to be natural and unaffected by the observation	Ethical issues might apply as participants do not know they are being observed. However, in a public place where they might expect to be observed, this is less unethical

Tallying

Tallying is used to get quantitative data in an observation. It involves making a mark when a particular behaviour is observed such as someone holding a door open for someone else.

Event sampling

Event sampling is when it is the event that is watched for and recorded, such as every time someone holds a door open for someone with a pushchair in a shopping centre.

Time sampling

Time sampling is when a record is made every so often, perhaps marking down what a child is doing every 2 minutes, for example.

Additional research methods and techniques

Twin and adoption studies

Twin studies

Twin studies use **monozygotic (MZ** — identical) twins and **dizygotic (DZ** — non-identical) twins on the principle that twins are brought up in a shared environment but MZ twins share 100% of their genes and DZ twins share 50% of their genes. A characteristic shared more in MZ twins than in DZ twins is said to be to a large extent down to nature (genes).

> **Questions & Answers**
>
> Issues and debates Role of nature and nurture in psychology Q1 looks at the nature-nurture debate focusing on what it means, and giving two examples to help to define it. Twin studies are one of the two examples offered including Brendgen et al. (2005) as an example of a twin study.

However, twins do not share 100% of their environment as both MZ and DZ twins might be in different school classes or be treated differently by their parents.

Adoption studies

Children who are adopted share their genes with their biological parents and their environment with their adoptive family so **adoption studies** can be useful when looking at nature versus nurture as well. If an adopted child shows characteristics relating to their biological family such characteristics might be seen as 'nature', coming from genes, and not 'nurture', coming from the environment. However, children can be adopted by relatives or families similar to their own, which can affect findings.

Exam tip

You should use these terms in your exam answers. For example, if you are given the scenario of an observation study and asked to suggest how data might be recorded, you can refer to event and time sampling, tallying and whether the observer is covert, overt, participant or non-participant.

Knowledge check 10

What is the advantage of using a covert non-participant observation?

Exam tip

For each research method you need to know about in your course, aim to know at least one example of a study using that method as that can help to show your understanding as well as your knowledge.

Animal experiments

Experiments using animals have the same features as experiments using humans to a large extent. An independent variable is manipulated to see the result in a dependent variable. There are **controls** over all other variables and the study is done usually in a controlled and artificial setting. Animals, however, are used in ways that humans are not, such as selective breeding of rats to look at the effects of certain characteristics or using **lesioning** in rats or mice to see the effects of such brain damage.

Animal studies can be useful in isolating factors for study, like brain areas, that cannot be studied in the same way in humans (such as the amygdala). However, there is a problem with generalising from animals to humans, given their differences, such as in problem solving.

Case studies as used in different areas in psychology

Case studies are in depth and detailed studies of one person or a small group. They tend to focus on qualitative data, but they can use quantitative data too. They often use different methods within them, such as observation, questionnaire and researching someone's history. They tend to have validity because they focus on someone's 'real life', and they can show reliability because triangulation can be done using data from the different methods. **Triangulation** involves checking data from different sources.

You have covered information about case studies in cognitive psychology such as the case of Henry Molaison. Freud also used case studies to develop his theory, which you might have looked at, and case studies are used in clinical psychology too. An example of a case study in clinical psychology that you might have studied is Lavarenne et al. (2013), when they wrote up a group session where those with psychosis were helped with their boundaries.

Scanning (CAT, PET, fMRI)

You need to know about CAT, PET and fMRI scanning as research methods, though there are other scanning (**neuroimaging**) techniques as well.

CAT

CAT scanning is computerised axial tomography and CT is X-ray computed tomography —both are the same except for the 'axial' component. This type of scanning can show bones and soft tissue, including in the brain.

PET

PET scanning is positron emission tomography which gives a three-dimensional image of the body's working. This is 'functional' imaging, which means a functioning brain can be looked at, which is different from CAT scanning. PET scanning uses a radionuclide that emits positrons (a tracer) and then the concentration of the tracer in the body is measured and mapped using a computer. High radioactivity means brain activity and the flow of blood to parts of the brain is measured so brain activity is measured.

Exam tip

Be ready to evaluate all the methods and methodology in your course, including the use of animal experiments to study human behaviour and characteristics.

Exam tip

When using animals in experiments there are both practical and ethical issues to consider. Be ready to discuss these and to deal with them separately too, in case a question focuses on one in particular.

Knowledge check 11

What are two practical issues that have to be considered when using animals in experiments?

Exam tip

Draw up a table comparing how case studies are used in different areas of psychology. Then draw up a table of the strengths and weaknesses of using the case study research method. Tables can help with revision, as can making comparisons.

---

fMRI

fMRI is functional magnetic resonance imaging and brain activity is measured by looking for changes in oxygen in the blood due to the activity of neurons in the brain (using magnets). An active part of the brain uses more oxygen.

Strengths and weaknesses of neuroimaging

Scanning is relatively non-invasive which is an advantage, and fMRI does not involve radiation, which means it is safe. A problem with CAT scanning is X-ray use, as X-rays should not be done often. Also CAT scans do not show brain functioning, just problems with brain tissue. PET scanning shows brain activity, which is useful for many purposes including seeing how the brain works, but it is relatively expensive and only gives a certain amount of detail and time-span. fMRI is also quite expensive and limited in time-span, such as an image of a whole brain being limited to being done only every 2 seconds.

Content analysis

Content analysis is a basic term for analysing some content such as text, video, drawings or TV advertisements to look for themes and categories and counting them to summarise what is said.

- **Summative content analysis** means looking for key words and counting them.
- **Conventional content analysis** is where categories are picked out from the data without a theory in mind.
- **Directive content analysis** is when theory drives the categories that are looked for.

Correlation research

Questions & Answers

Methods Unseen study: a questionnaire Q1b refers to Likert-ranked data, ordinal data, and a correlation. Q1c also refers to a positive correlation.

One main means of collecting and understanding data is to use **correlation design**. When a relationship between variables is looked for a correlation is focused on. (When looking for a difference between variables, that means a test of difference.)

When a score on one variable rises as a score on another variable rises, so there is a clear relationship between them, that means there is a **positive correlation**. A perfect positive correlation means a score on a test of +1. For example, reaction time rises (it takes longer to react) as people get older (as age rises). A correlation shows **covariables**, which are variables that change together.

When a score on one variable rises as a score on another variable falls, this also shows a clear relationship, a **negative correlation**. A perfect negative correlation means a score on a test of −1. For example, driving speed in mph falls as people get older (age rises).

When scores on two variables do not relate at all, that means there is no correlation. No correlation means a score of 0 on a test. The sales of bread in a supermarket may have no relationship to the weather temperature, for example.

When a correlation is close to 1 (either –1 or +1) it is a strong correlation. The **strength of the correlation** is how near it is to a perfect correlation.

Longitudinal and cross-sectional designs

Longitudinal

Longitudinal studies are where one or more participants are researched over time and scores noted so that their development over time can be charted. As the same people are used, participant variables are controlled for, though people can drop out which can affect the representativeness of a sample.

Cross-sectional

Cross-sectional studies are where different groups are studied at one moment in time, such as people in different age groups being studied together. Then there can be comparisons about development over time but not using the same people. This is quicker than using longitudinal methods and people do not drop out, but participant differences might affect results.

Cross-cultural design

Cross-cultural methods involve using participants in different cultures so that they can be compared to look for similarities and differences between cultures. **Universality** can be studied as if a result is found in many different cultures, this might mean it is in our nature and a 'universal law'. The same procedure is used in a set of cross-cultural studies so that only the culture varies. One problem is that a procedure might not work in the same way in different cultures so might not be similarly understood, which might affect the findings rather than culture itself (e.g. different experiences) affecting the findings. The strange situation, mentioned when looking at structured observation (page 19), has been used cross-culturally.

The use of meta-analysis using cross-cultural research and the universality of attachment types

Meta-analyses involve using the findings of different studies that have used the same or a very similar research method so that the findings can be pooled. This gives a larger sample and more findings, hopefully showing reliability and generalisability.

> **Exam tip**
>
> Look through your course to find a meta-analysis. If you covered child psychology then your classic study was a meta-analysis using a cross-cultural design. Stafford et al. (2015) carried out a meta-analysis to look at treatments of psychosis and schizophrenia.

Exam tip

The strength of a correlation is different from how significant the result of a correlation is (page 26), though they are linked. Use the specification to see the terms you need to understand for Topic 9.

Knowledge check 13

What is a main difference between longitudinal and cross-sectional designs?

Exam tip

Use examples when explaining longitudinal, cross-sectional and cross-cultural designs. Examples you used in clinical psychology would be suitable, e.g. Hankin et al. (1998) looked at depression, gender and how depression arises in young people, which is a longitudinal design. The classic study in child psychology uses cross-cultural data.

If a meta-analysis using cross-cultural data finds similar data from studies using similar methods in different cultures then what is found might show universality, which means it is down to human nature and not to learning. For example, if similar attachment types are found in all cultures where they are studied this suggests those attachment types are universal.

Control issues

Many control issues that arise when doing research in psychology have already been covered in this section on research methods. You need to know about:

- demand characteristics (page 19)
- experimenter effects (page 17)
- social desirability (page 14)
- participant and situational variables (page 16)
- extraneous and confounding variables (page 16)
- counterbalancing (page 10)
- order effects (page 10)
- operationalisation of variables (page 12)

> **Exam tip**
>
> Create mnemonics to help your recall. 'Despecoo' for this list sounds like a word that you might relate to 'desperate'. You can probably think of something with personal meaning for you. Then in the exam you have the first letter of some terms, to help trigger recall.

Analysis of quantitative data: descriptive statistics

> **Questions & Answers**
>
> Review of studies Unseen studies Q1a refers to standard deviation and the spread of scores in an unseen study.

Descriptive statistics involve **measures of central tendency** — the **mean**, the **median** and the **mode** of a set of data. They also involve **measures of dispersion** — the **range** and **standard deviation** of a set of scores. These measures of dispersion show how scores vary around the mean, showing the spread of the scores. Descriptive statistics also involve graphs and tables. These are all ways of 'describing' the data.

Graphs you need to know about are **histograms**, **bar charts** and **scatter diagrams**. Tables you need to know about are **frequency tables**. You also need to know what raw data are (the actual scores) and how to draw up tables to display data (including displaying the mode, median, mean and range of data).

You also need to know about normal and skewed distribution as well as sense checking of data.

> **Exam tip**
>
> For each method issue you have to cover be sure to make a note of some strengths and weaknesses and evaluation points.

> **Knowledge check 14**
>
> Why is it so important to use controls to avoid bias in a piece of research?

- Data show **normal distribution** if the mean, median and mode are very similar and you would see a bell-shaped curve in a frequency graph and in normal distrubution the curve would be regular, with the highest part in the middle shown by the mean, median and mode.
- **Skewed distribution** is found if the data have more than one mode or the mean, median and mode are different (such as there being an **outlier** score).
- **Sense checking** of data means looking carefully at data before doing any inferential test. Descriptive statistics help with sense checking, such as seeing if there is an outlier score that skews the distribution of scores or seeing whether one condition has a lot more of the higher scores than another condition.
- You have to be able to produce, handle and interpret data including drawing comparisons between two (or more) sets of data and using sense checking is part of doing that.

Analysis of quantitative data: inferential statistics

Inferential statistics are used when data are quantitative to find out whether any difference between scores in different conditions or any relationship between scores is likely to be due to chance. There are various features of inferential testing that you need to know about.

Levels of measurement

Data can be measured using different **levels of measurement**:
- **Nominal data** are where categories are used such as 'aggressive' or 'not aggressive'.
- **Ordinal data** are when there is ranking such as scores on a scale of 1 to 5.
- **Interval/ratio data** are data where there is 'real' measurement such as the time or number of times something is done. The important point is that the scores have equal intervals/distances between them where rankings (ordinal data) might not.

> ### Questions & Answers
>
> Methods Unseen study: a questionnaire Q1b refers to ordinal data as coming from Likert-ranked data.

Choosing a statistical test

In your course you only need to know four **inferential tests**, though there are others. The four tests are given in Table 12 to help to show you how to choose the right test.

Table 12 Choosing an appropriate statistical test

Test of difference			Correlation
Experimental/ research design	Nominal data	Ordinal data (can be used for interval data too)	**Spearman's**
Repeated measures or matched pairs	*Not in your course*	**Wilcoxon**	
Independent groups	**Chi-squared**	**Mann–Whitney U**	

Knowledge check 15

In one set of scores, Scores A, the mean average was 5.5, the median was 4.5 and the mode was 2.5. In another set of scores, Scores B, the mean average was 7.8, the median was 7 and the mode was 8. Which of the two sets of scores would show normal distribution and which would show skewed distribution?

The formula for each of the four tests will be in the front of your exam paper to help you.

One-tailed or two-tailed

When looking up the significance of the result of one of the statistical tests you need to know whether to use a **one-tailed or two-tailed test/column**. A directional hypothesis (page 13) means **one-tailed** and a non-directional hypothesis (page 13) means **two-tailed**.

Levels of significance

To find out whether differences or relationships between conditions are significant, means to find out whether the difference or relationship is enough to show it is not due to chance.

- The null hypothesis (page 12) says the results will not be significantly different and the null hypothesis is tested using statistical tests. The question is whether any difference or relationship found is different enough to be said not to be due to chance.
- Results can be accepted if 5% of them are due to chance and 95% are not, or if 1% of them are due to chance and 99% are not. There are also other **levels of significance** that are accepted in psychology. A 10% likelihood of results being due to chance is not accepted.
- The way a 5% chance possibility is written is $p \leq .05$ which means the probability of results being due to chance (p) is equal to or less then ($\leq$) 5% (.05). $p \leq .01$ is how a 1% chance level is written and $p \leq .10$ is a 10% level of significance.

Questions & Answers

Methods Unseen study: a questionnaire: Q1a covers the meaning of 'p' and refers to accepting the alternate hypothesis. '$<$' is also explained, as is '.001'. Q1c also refers to the strength of the $p < .001$ finding.

- You need to be able to use levels of significance and inferential statistical testing to accept or reject the null hypothesis in a study and to state which hypothesis is accepted.

Critical and observed values

You will have been using the four tests when doing the practical investigations for your course and when learning about them.

- You will have found the resulting statistic for each test: T for Wilcoxon, U for Mann–Whitney, ρ/r_s for Spearman's and χ^2 for Chi-squared.

Exam tip

You can be asked to do these tests in the exam and you are given the formulae in the front of each paper. Practise doing each of the four tests.

Knowledge check 16

If a study looks for a difference and uses an independent groups design with nominal data gathered, what test is suitable?

Exam tip

Be ready to be given a study and then asked questions about it, including for a set of results what inferential test would be suitable and why. Use Table 12 to help you choose the right one.

Exam tip

Draw up a table that includes as many terms as you can remember from Section A so far and then write a definition of each term. Check your table both for inclusion of all necessary terms and for accuracy of your definitions.

Exam tip

Now draw up another list of any terms you missed in response to the previous exam tip. Then aim to define them. Keep reviewing and revising in this sort of way to help your learning. You can use the glossary to help.

- The result of the test can be seen as the **observed/calculated value** though the Chi-squared test has the 'observed' value as something specific so watch out for that.
- The way you see whether the result of a test is significant or not is to compare it with a critical value using **critical values tables**. The critical values tables you need are in the specification and in the front of each exam paper. Also given with the tables is the information about whether you need the observed/calculated value (the result of the test) to be equal to or more than the critical value, less than the critical value and so on for there to be significance.
- To use critical values tables you need:
  (a) the result of the test you have done
  (b) whether you need a one- or a two-tailed column
  (c) the level of significance you have chosen or are given
  (d) sometimes you need to know **N**, which is the number of participants
  (e) for the Chi-squared you need to know the **degrees of freedom (df)**, which is 1 for a two-by-two table

Exam tip

Look carefully at all the critical values tables in the specification. Get used to which tests ask for the test result to be equal to or more than the critical value and look at which need N and which need df.

Accepting and rejecting the null, Type I and Type II errors

When you have compared the result of a statistical test with the critical value using critical values tables, you will know whether the result was significant or not. You will have chosen the level of significance beforehand. For example, for 10 participants at $p<.05$ when a hypothesis is directional (one-tailed) the result of a Spearman's test must be 0.442 or greater. If your result from doing a Spearman's test is 0.56 then you have a significant result and you reject the null hypothesis, claiming the results of your study were not due to chance. The alternate hypothesis is accepted.

You will not know more until someone else repeats your study or does a similar one. If they do not find significant results, they might suggest that there was a **Type I error** in your study and say that you chose an optimistic level of significance (accepting that 5% of your results might be due to chance). Alternatively, in another study not getting significant results, you might have used a $p<.001$ level of significance thinking that just 1 result in 1000 would be due to chance. If the follow-up study to this found significance at $p<.01$ but not at $p<.001$ it might suggest you made a **Type II** error in wrongly choosing too difficult a level of significance.

Knowledge check 17

If you find by using critical values tables that the result of a statistical test is not significant, do you accept or reject the null hypothesis?

Exam tip

You might want to learn what these terms mean by rote. For example, learn that a Type I error means wrongly rejecting the null hypothesis (wrongly saying the study 'worked'), and learn that a Type II error means wrongly accepting the null hypothesis (wrongly saying the study did not 'work').

Methodological issues (evaluation)

So far this section has covered how studies are carried out and analysed. You will know that an important point when designing and considering studies is to be sceptical and to consider strengths and weaknesses along the way. There are several specific evaluation issues that you can focus on. These are validity, reliability, generalisability, objectivity-subjectivity and credibility. These are briefly reviewed here.

Content Guidance

Validity

You can talk about validity when considering studies in psychology. It means that what is being measured is what is said to have been measured. For example, if Baddeley (1966b) is studying short-term and long-term memory then his conclusions seem of interest, but he starts with the idea that there are these two stores, which might not be a valid assumption.

Internal

You can also talk about specific types of validity, one of which is **internal validity**. This refers to research methods that claim cause-and-effect results, like experiments. If extraneous variables are controlled for and there are no confounding variables, then there is internal validity. Internal validity refers to when a cause-and-effect conclusion is justified.

Predictive

Another type of validity you need to know about is **predictive validity**, which refers to measures on a scale or such scores, such as when using a questionnaire. Results have predictive validity if later reality relates to what was found in the study. For example, if a test to find a suitable job applicant has predictive validity, that means that the person doing the job does well and is found to be suitable after a year in the job.

Ecological

Ecological validity is also named in your course. Results have ecological validity if what is done relates to the real world. The setting of the study should be 'real life' and what is done should match 'real life' too. For example, memory experiments may not represent memory in real-life situations.

Reliability

There are several types of reliability but your course is not specific. You need to know that reliability is found in results when they are found again when the study is repeated. Results that are consistent are reliable.

Generalisability

Results of a study can be evaluated in terms of their generalisability. If results are said to be true of a target population when a sample does not represent that population then the results are wrongly generalised. Usually results must be generalisable for policy and practice to come from them (though case studies that are unique and about one person can have value).

Objectivity and subjectivity

Results need **objectivity** to be scientific and to have credibility. They must not be affected by personal opinion or bias, which would be subjectivity. Researcher bias in terms of subjectivity, such as in what is being looked for, which can affect results, is to be avoided.

Credibility

A credible researcher is one who is accepted as knowledgeable in their field and with expertise that can be trusted. There is also **credibility** in data that have good controls where there is no bias in the results.

Improving studies in psychology

- You can use discussion of the various methodology issues (e.g. validity, reliability, generalisability, objectivity-subjectivity and credibility, as well as ethics) to propose ways of improving studies in psychology. For example, experiments tend to be reliable as they can be repeated so reliability can be tested, whereas case studies tend to be valid, because they enter someone's real-life world.
- You will be asked to make suggestions about improving studies so it is useful to practise doing this.
- You could use other method issues such as suggesting a change in the design from repeated measures to independent groups to avoid order effects.

Questions & Answers

Methods Unseen study: an animal laboratory experiment Q1d refers to how to suggest ways in which an unseen study can be improved.

Exam tip

Check your understanding of the evaluation issues listed in this section. Make sure you can give an example of each to discuss in an exam question.

Exam tip

Use the sample assessment material (on the Edexcel website), go through all the unseen studies and suggest ways to improve them, to practise that skill.

Knowledge check 19

A study used a laboratory experiment with a repeated measures design to see whether people remembered more 'office' equipment if taken into an office than if taken into a library. Recall was in another room. Suggest one way of improving the study.

Analysis of qualitative data

Thematic analysis is used to analyse qualitative data and you need to know about grounded theory as well. It may seem as if there is more focus on use of quantitative data in your course, for various reasons, including the required focus on research methods and on historic issues around 'doing science', but qualitative data also have value and must be analysed.

Thematic analysis

Qualitative data are in the form of a story, a picture or a video, or something like that. Analysis of such data is done by deriving themes from the data. This is thematic analysis. There are various steps laid down for using **thematic analysis**, from the **transcript**, which is the whole data presented ready for analysis, through generating initial codes to defining and naming themes and presenting them as results.

Grounded theory

A main difference with **grounded theory** as a way of analysing qualitative data, compared with thematic analysis, is that the theory is 'grounded' in the data, meaning the theory comes out of the analysis. Researchers using a grounded theory approach would not have a theory, their research question would be more open. They would hope that theory would arise from their data.

Table 13 Strengths and weaknesses of thematic analysis and grounded theory as ways of analysing qualitative data

Means of analysis of qualitative data	Strengths	Weaknesses
Thematic analysis	Can search for patterns in the data but unlike grounded theory does not need to have theory derived from the data so can suit wider purposes — such as everyday experience of reality. Also can be used within different theoretical frameworks	An individual develops themes from a text and the analysis can be strong or less strong depending on the ability of the individual. Also it is hard to separate thematic analysis from content analysis in some ways — it is not an easy method to pin down
Grounded theory	Useful for studying new areas and understanding new phenomena and useful for helping the researcher(s) keep an open mind when analysing	There will be a lot of data and analysis will be slow (as will data collection). Not having theory to drive a research question means grounded theory is limited in its use

> **Exam tip**
> Write a short paragraph about why you think there is more focus on quantitative data than on qualitative data in your course. Focus on psychology as science, on validity versus reliability and objectivity in your consideration of the issue. This will help you to learn issues.

> **Exam tip**
> The strengths and weaknesses of ways of analysing qualitative data are considered here. This has not been done for all the methodology issues in this Content section, but it would be useful for you to draw up such tables to help with your revision.

> **Knowledge check 20**
> Give an example of when grounded theory might be a useful approach to studying an area in psychology.

Conventions of published psychological research

You need to know how research in psychology is disseminated to people who need to know about it. A main way is to publish a paper/article in a journal and to do that a piece of research written up as a report must have a scholarly peer review (also known as 'refereeing'). **Peer reviewing** means the research paper is sent to experts in the field of study so that they can scrutinise what was done. In this way what is published in journals is vetted for its suitability, usefulness and soundness.

A **report** in psychology has to follow a set structure and it is published as an article. The structure involves a title, an **abstract** where the whole study is summarised, and an **introduction** giving background of other studies in the field of study and ending with a research question, hypotheses and **aims**. A **method** section follows, which gives information about participants, the design used, any apparatus/materials and the procedure. **Results** follow the method section, then there is a **discussion**, followed by references giving information about all the other work that is cited and appendices come at the end if there are any.

Ethical issues in research using humans

Questions & Answers

Review of studies Unseen studies Q1c considers ethics as a weakness of an unseen study.

You need to know about the British Psychological Society's Code of Ethics and Conduct (2009) as well as risk management. You will also have looked at guidelines of the Health and Care Professions Council (HCPC) in clinical psychology. All psychologists (working as psychologists) must be registered with the HCPC to call themselves 'psychologists' such as forensic and clinical psychologists. In the methods part of Paper 3 your focus must be on the BPS Code and on risk management.

BPS Code of Ethics and Conduct (2009)

The BPS Code has four principles relating to **ethics** in research (and in the practice of psychology). These are respect, responsibility, integrity and competence:

- **Respect** includes keeping records, respecting difference, maintaining **confidentiality** as appropriate, obtaining **informed consent** and avoiding unnecessary **deception**. Giving the **right to withdraw** also falls under the principle of respect.
- **Responsibility** refers to the avoidance of harm and links to issues about the right to withdraw (such as that it is still a participant's right to do so even if payment is involved). Giving a **debrief** also links to responsibility.
- **Integrity** refers to psychologists being honest and accurate and maintaining personal boundaries with clients. Colleagues must be challenged with regard to their ethics as part of the principle of integrity.
- **Competence** relates to a psychologist recognising ethical problems, accepting responsibility for any dilemmas, and keeping within the limits of competence as well as maintaining competence.

Risk management

Risk management is an important part of doing research in psychology. You should review the notes you made about risk management when you covered that area in social psychology.

Exam tip

You need to know what sections there are in a report in psychology, such as 'method' and 'results'. Be ready to say what each section involves and also to explain the process of peer review.

Exam tip

You could access one of the studies in your course to see how a report is written up.

Knowledge check 21

Explain why peer reviewing is important in psychology when publishing studies.

Knowledge check 22

Explain the ethical principle of competence using two of its features.

Exam tip

For each ethical principle prepare an example from studies you have covered, such as considering whether Little Albert (Watson and Rayner, 1920) had the right to withdraw and considering the debrief used in Milgram (1963).

Ethical issues in research using animals

The Animals (Scientific Procedures) Act 1986 gives rules about using animals in laboratory experiments and in research using animals in general. The rules are backed by Home Office licensing.

Exam tip

Be ready for an extended writing question about ethical issues when using animals in research in psychology as well as an unseen study asking about such issues. Prepare studies as examples of the use of animals and related ethical issues too, such as Pavlov's work with dogs.

Exam tip

Check your understanding of the rules for using animals, such as the researcher having a licence and the place the study takes place in also having a licence, as well as the animals being the right ones and not endangered.

Summary: methods

You need to know the following:

- types of data (qualitative and quantitative data) and sampling techniques (random; stratified; volunteer; and opportunity)
- experimental/research designs (independent groups; repeated measures; matched pairs) and hypotheses (null; alternate; experimental; directional and non-directional)
- questionnaires and interviews (open, closed and rank-scale questions; structured, semi-structured and unstructured interviews; self-report data)
- experiments (lab and field; independent and dependent variables) and observations (tallying; event and time sampling; covert, overt, participant and non-participant; structured and naturalistic)
- additional research methods and techniques (twin and adoption studies; animal experiments; case studies in different areas in psychology; scanning — fMRI, PET and CAT; content analysis; correlation research; longitudinal and cross-sectional; cross-cultural; meta-analysis)
- control issues (counterbalancing and order effects; experimenter effects, social desirability and demand characteristics; participant and situational variables; extraneous and confounding variables; operationalisation of variables)
- descriptive statistics (measures of central tendency; frequency tables; graphs — bar chart, histogram, scatter diagram; normal distribution, skewed distribution and standard deviation;

sense checking data; measures of dispersion — range, standard deviation). Also being able to produce, handle and interpret data including drawing comparisons (no need to know the formulae but must be able to do the maths)
- inferential statistics (levels of measurement; choice of statistical test; criteria for Mann–Whitney U-test, Wilcoxon, Spearman's and Chi-squared; directional and non-directional testing; use of critical value tables and one- and two-tailed testing; levels of significance; rejecting hypotheses; Type I and Type II errors; p values and levels of significance; observed/calculated and critical values). No need to know the formulae but must be able to do the maths
- methodological issues: validity (internal, predictive, ecological); reliability; generalisability; objectivity and subjectivity (researcher bias); credibility
- analysis of qualitative data (thematic analysis and grounded theory)
- conventions of published psychological research (abstract; introduction; aims and hypotheses; method; results; discussion; the process of peer review)
- ethical issues in research using humans (BPS Code of Ethics and Conduct, 2009; risk assessment when carrying out research in psychology)
- ethical issues in research using animals (Scientific Procedures Act, 1986 and Home Office regulations)

■ Section B: Review of studies

You need to be able to review the studies you have covered throughout your course, in particular classic studies. You covered one classic study each in social, cognitive and biological psychology as well as learning theories and clinical psychology, so five classic studies in all. You will also have covered a classic study in your choice of application from criminological, child and health psychology though that is not reviewed here. You have also covered a compulsory contemporary study when looking at Carlsson et al. (1999/2000), which looks at schizophrenia in clinical psychology.

In Section B there is:

- a section on reviewing the classic studies
- a section where classic studies must be related to the 11 issues and debates in your course
- a section to test your understanding of issues in studies you have not seen before (unseen studies), including testing your evaluation skills and your skills of drawing on different areas and having an overview of your course (**synoptic** skills)

Classic studies: draw on and compare

The classic studies in your course are: Sherif et al. (1954/1961); Baddeley (1966b); Raine et al. (1997); Watson and Rayner (1920); and Rosenhan (1973).

Sherif et al. (1954/1961)

Sherif et al. carried out the Robbers Cave study where two groups of boys were set up without knowing about one another, using a summer camp situation. When the boys found out about one another they entered into competition and there was prejudice between the two groups. When the two groups had to work together to achieve goals they both needed to achieve, to an extent prejudice was reduced.

Baddeley (1966b)

Baddeley set out to see whether long-term memory used an acoustic store as he had found out short-term memory did. He found that long-term memory was affected by the meaning of words so thought storage in long-term memory was not acoustic but semantic. He took this as evidence that there were the two separate stores. The study was a laboratory experiment.

Raine et al. (1997)

Raine et al. studied people who were undergoing a PET scan as part of their defense 'not guilty by reason of insanity'. They put together a control group matched in many ways, who underwent PET scanning as well. Then they compared the scans of the 'murderers' against the controls and found there were differences in their brains in the areas related to aggression.

> **Exam tip**
>
> It is hard to prepare for Paper 3 as questions will be asking you to draw on different parts of your course. You can practise by drawing up tables comparing different elements such as biological explanations across your course or when learning theories are used, or issues within the classic studies.

> **Knowledge check 23**
>
> Compare Baddeley (1966b) and Raine et al. (1997) in terms of two issues relating to their procedure.

Watson and Rayner (1920)

Watson and Rayner (1920) used a young baby they called 'Little Albert' to see if they could condition a fear in him. They made sure he was not afraid of a pet rat and then made a loud noise over Little Albert's head to frighten him. When they paired the frightening noise with the pet rat, after a few pairings the boy showed fear and distress when the pet rat was near. The researchers felt they had conditioned a fear through the process of classical conditioning and they showed generalisation of the fear too, as the boy showed distress when presented with things similar to the rat.

Rosenhan (1973)

Rosenhan used 8 participants to visit 12 hospitals, one presenting themselves at each hospital. They said they heard 'thud' or 'hollow' in their heads and apart from that each person gave 'true' information about themselves. They were admitted to the hospital on the basis of this one 'symptom' and found it hard to persuade the hospital staff of their 'normality' once they were admitted. This was taken to show validity issues with the diagnosis of mental disorder.

Questions & Answers

Review of studies Classic studies Q1a looks at comparing Rosenhan's (1973) procedure with Loftus and Palmer's (1974) procedure. Loftus and Palmer is the classic study for criminological psychology (you may not have chosen that option).

Questions & Answers

Review of studies Classic studies Q1b considers what makes a classic study 'classic', referring to Watson and Rayner (1920).

Classic studies: issues and debates

The 11 issues and debates are outlined briefly in Section C of this content guidance section. You need to be able to relate the classic studies to the issues and debates. Table 14 gives some ideas for how the classic studies can be related to the different issues and debates and you can build on these ideas.

Questions & Answers

Review of studies Classic studies: issues and debates Q1a relates Rosenhan (1973) and Baddeley (1966b) to the issue and debate about how psychological understanding has developed over time. It also refers to how quantitative data tend to come from a more scientific method.

Knowledge check 24

Show how two classic studies in your course use the laboratory experimental method.

Exam tip

You need to be able to compare the classic studies and to draw on them. Table 14 gives ideas how to relate the classic studies to issues and debates. You could use tables in a similar way, such as to relate their research methods, their sampling or their generalisability.

Table 14 Relating the classic studies to the 11 issues and debates: some ideas

Classic study	Issues and debates	Some ideas
Sherif et al. (1954/1961)	Gender	The study looked only at boys. There is no suggestion that the findings related only to boys, but you could argue that generalising the findings to girls might not be suitable
	Practical issues in the design of research	The researchers took some trouble with the participants so that the two groups matched to some extent and comparing them was then possible. This was a practical issue in the design, as was keeping the two groups apart so that they did not know about each other at first
	Comparison of themes	This study might help regarding comparing themes as it illustrates both social identity theory and realistic conflict theory as theories of prejudice
Baddeley (1966b)	Psychology as science	Baddeley had done previous work showing that short-term memory used acoustic coding and he built on it in this study, building a body of knowledge. He used lab experiments and controls, to draw cause-and-effect conclusions, showing psychology as science
	The development of psychological understanding over time	Baddeley (with Hitch) went on to develop different ways of looking at short-term memory, showing how psychological understanding develops over time
Raine et al. (1997)	Ethics Socially sensitive research	The participants were pleading not guilty by reason of insanity. Showing their brains were dysfunctional in areas relating to aggression might be used in their defense, to help, but there is an implication of whether this removes responsibility from them
	Psychology as science	This was a scientific study in that there was a control group, matched in important ways, so that cause-and-effect conclusions could be claimed
Watson and Rayner (1920)	Reductionism	Reducing 'phobia' to showing distress when a scary noise is paired with a previously liked object/animal might not represent a 'real' phobia, which may have more than one 'cause'
	Psychology as science	The study is scientific in that they controlled the environment and what was present in it when the noise was given
	Nature-nurture	There were nurture issues in that the boy learned a phobia — it was learned from his experiences
	Using psychology in society	If classical conditioning can be shown to produce an association of a fear response then the principles might be helpful in cancelling a fear response. This is an illustration of using psychology in society
Rosenhan (1973)	Socially sensitive research	Diagnosing mental disorders is a socially sensitive area, especially as this study showed diagnosis was by no means secure
	Social control	There is an element of social control shown when the researchers could not persuade the staff that they did not have a mental disorder

Exam tip

All 11 issues and debates are touched on in Table 14, but you need to know more about each in relation to the classic studies so go through each issue and debate and write down as much as you can about how the classic studies help to illustrate each issue.

Knowledge check 25

Use two classic studies to raise issues about reductionism in psychology.

Exam tip

Issues and debates can be used to evaluate the classic studies, such as to help with strengths and weaknesses. For example, it can be a strength if a study is scientific in its approach, but you would need to say why this is a strength.

Unseen studies: understanding, evaluation and synopticity

The final part of Section B of the psychological skills part of your course is for you to be presented with studies you have not seen before and answer questions about them. You need to be able to evaluate them and draw together ideas from your course that can help to shed light on an unseen study or to assess or discuss it.

Questions & Answers

Methods Unseen study: a questionnaire Q1c uses an unseen study and asks how the findings can be evidence for social identity theory. This is an example of how an unseen study must be linked to a theory you have learned about.

Exam tip

Find studies using the internet or use the studies in the sample assessment materials or past papers. Write about these 'unseen' studies in terms of evaluation issues (e.g. reliability, validity, generalisability, credibility, subjectivity/objectivity and ethics). Also explain the study in your own words to help to show understanding.

Questions & Answers

Review of studies Unseen studies Q1b uses an unseen study and relates the findings to theory in the course so tests synopticity.

Questions & Answers

Review of studies Unseen studies Q1c considers strengths and weaknesses of an unseen study.

Knowledge check 26

Use classic studies to show how psychology can relate to issues around social control.

Knowledge check 27

A study showed that people with semantic dementia (dementia not coming from hippocampus loss) were better at more recent memories and those with hippocampus loss were better at recalling their long-term memories. What does this study show about the hippocampus?

Knowledge check 28

An animal laboratory study found that animals conditioned to take heroin in response to drug cues could have their association weakened by the cues not being present. Extinction can take place. The neurobiological mechanisms involved in the extinction seem similar to those in the extinction of fear which might help to encourage extinction of drug habits in humans, by using known ways of extinguishing a fear response. Explain a weakness of this study.

Summary: review of studies

- In Year 1 there are four classic studies: Sherif et al. (1954/1961); Baddeley (1966b); Raine et al. (1997); Watson and Rayner (1920).
- In Year 2 clinical psychology has Rosenhan (1973) as the classic study and each of the three option applications has a classic study.
- Topic 9 requires a review of classic studies, including comparing them and drawing on them to answer questions.
- Topic 9 also requires 11 issues and debates to be covered (Section C) and in Section B asks for a synoptic review of the classic studies in terms of the issues and debates in the course.
- A final section of Section B in Topic 9 involves the use of unseen studies to show understanding, evaluation and synopticity.

■ Section C: Issues and debates

You need to review 11 issues and debates. You will need to discuss the issues and debates in relation to material in Papers 1, 2 and 3. The 11 issues and debates are outlined briefly in this section to help your revision.

> **Exam tip**
>
> You could generate an essay title for each issue to prepare/ practise an answer. For example, in the title 'Assess how far there are (XXX) in psychological research' you could substitute the different issues and debates. Change the wording a little if you need to.

Ethical issues in research (animal and human)

You will have revised ethical issues in research both relating to the use of animals and humans. With regard to the use of animals, you can use the Scientific Procedures Act (1986). With regard to the use of humans you can use the BPS Code of Ethics and Conduct (2009), issues around the management of risk, and you can draw on what you learned about HCPC guidelines for clinical psychology too. If you have covered child psychology you can bring in issues around a child's rights.

> **Exam tip**
>
> When discussing ethics and animals in studies avoid any mention of human guidelines such as giving the right to withdraw and focus on the ethics of using animals in studies such as avoiding endangered species and caring for the animals in a suitable way.

Practical issues in the design and implementation of research

Throughout your course you have been studying method issues. You have also carried out a number of practical investigations. You will have been considering practical issues in the design and implementation of research. For example, issues include problems with order effects if a repeated measures design is used, and how to overcome these effects such as using counterbalancing as a practical solution. Practical issues can include how to operationalise variables to get a measurable dependent variable, such as how to measure driving behaviour perhaps.

Reductionism in the explanation of behaviour

You covered the idea of **reductionism** when you learned about psychology as science in the learning theories part of your course in Year 1. Review your material on reductionism so that you can discuss it as an issue and debate. Reductionism refers to reducing something to measurable manageable parts so that it can be studied. The issue is that by doing so the 'whole' is lost and not studied. Studying the 'whole' is

> **Exam tip**
>
> Be ready to discuss each of the issues and debates using examples from your course. Section C of psychological skills (Paper 3) includes a 20-mark essay/piece of extended writing, so be ready to respond to an issues and debates question of that length and style.

> **Knowledge check 29**
>
> Explain one ethical issue with regard to one study using human participants that you have covered.

> **Knowledge check 30**
>
> Explain ethical issues with regard to one study using animals that you have covered.

> **Exam tip**
>
> To prepare an answer about practical issues when doing research, make a list of possible issues including the two ideas suggested in this section.

> **Knowledge check 31**
>
> Why do you think Rosenhan (1973) had his participants give information truthfully except for the 'thud' and 'hollow' sounds they had to say they heard?

called a **holistic** approach. A strength of using a reductionist approach is that there can be controlled study of those manageable parts and the understanding gained can be useful. For example, understanding brain functioning relating to aggression as Raine et al. (1997) did can be valuable.

Exam tip

It can be said that reductionist research is limited because it misses the whole picture, but you can use the point as a strength of research because by being reductionist and focusing on a specific part of a behaviour, for example, controls are more possible, giving cause-and-effect results.

Knowledge check 32

Is a piece of research gathering qualitative data more likely to be taking a holistic or a reductionist approach?

Comparisons of explaining behaviour using different themes

Different themes are used in psychology to explain behaviour. There are main perspectives such as behaviourism and Freud's psychodynamic approach, which can be seen as themes. There are themes within such perspectives/approaches as well, such as the theme of group decision making in social psychology and the themes of culture and gender in psychological research, relating to explaining behaviour. You need to be able to compare such themes in relation to how they explain behaviour.

Questions & Answers

Issues and debates Comparisons of ways of explaining behaviour using different themes Q1 focuses on the strengths and weaknesses of two different themes used to explain behaviour relating to schizophrenia.

Exam tip

Check on the approaches/perspectives (e.g. social and cognitive psychology) so that you can use them as themes. Within each of the larger perspectives/approaches see what themes you can find. Then compare them, perhaps in relation to specific behaviour such as aggression or behaviour related to a mental disorder.

Knowledge check 33

Aggression can be studied using different themes/ approaches. Give three different themes you encountered in your study of aggression in your course.

Psychology as a science

You covered the idea of psychology as science in the learning theories part of your course in Year 1. You looked at issues of reductionism, replicability, reliability, validity (internal, predictive and ecological validity), falsification, empiricism, hypothesis testing and the use of controls. Some of these features of science and of psychology being less scientific have been covered in Section A of this guide: replicability, reliability, the three types of validity, hypothesis testing and the use of controls. Reductionism is an issue and debate of its own as you have seen. The other features of psychology as science — falsification and empiricism — are explained briefly here.

Questions & Answers

Review of studies Classic studies Q1a an answer evaluating the procedures of Rosenhan (1973) and Loftus and Palmer (1974) mentions objectivity, replicability, generalisability, validity and 'science'.

Falsification is a feature of science. The idea (from Karl Popper) is that researchers should aim to falsify a hypothesis rather than to find evidence for the hypothesis. The point is that we cannot 'prove' anything to be 'true', we can only show with certainty that something is false. We can keep testing a hypothesis such as 'all females are better driver than males' and find lots of times that this is the case (this is just an example of course), but that would not prove the statement true. As soon as we find one better male driver we have proved the statement false. This is what science is about — trying to prove statements false. In practice, psychology tends to add up the evidence 'for' a hypothesis rather than 'proving' it false.

Empiricism refers to getting data from our senses — sight, sound, touch, taste and smell.

The cycle of 'doing **science**' is: an hypothesis is generated from a **theory**, empirical data are collected (using our senses, from reality) and if the hypothesis seems to be supported, the theory is said to be supported.

Questions & Answers

Review of studies Classic studies: issues and debates Q1a relates Rosenhan (1973) and Baddeley (1966b) to psychology as a science, including mentioning how quantitative data tend to come from a more scientific method.

Exam tip

Research methods like using case studies or getting data from children by listening and engaging with them have value but can be called 'unscientific'. Such research in psychology still focuses on avoiding bias, including subjectivity on the part of the researcher. There is an element of science involved.

Culture and gender issues in psychological research

You have looked at **culture** to see if it affects obedience and seen that obedience seems to be more a response to the situation than coming from someone's cultural background. **Gender** also featured in studies of obedience, also showing that obedience comes from the situation rather than being affected by gender. However, it did seem that gender affected the participant's emotional responses in Milgram's studies. Females seemed more distressed by having to obey against their moral code.

Exam tip

The status of psychology as science is an important issue because science tends to be accepted as the way of knowing about our world and psychology is about knowing about mind and behaviour. You might be asked about how far a piece of research is scientific.

Knowledge check 34

Why are empirical data gathered to test a hypothesis (which has been derived from theory)? In Pavlov's (1927) work give an example of empirical data that were gathered.

Gather up more information from your course about gender and culture issues so that you are ready to answer a question on either issue.

Questions & Answers

Issues and debates Gender issues in psychological research Q1 focuses on describing gender issues in one area of psychology in the course. Obedience is chosen as the area.

Exam tip

Prepare answers on both culture and gender as variables in research in psychology so that you have some ideas. In the exam when you start writing using the ideas you have, it is likely that other ideas will then come, but it is useful to have some prepared ideas to start with.

The role of both nature and nurture in psychology

You covered twin studies in biological psychology. They also feature in the review of research methods in Section A of this content guidance section. Twin studies relate to the study of the effects of nature and of the environment on our behaviour and characteristics. Twin studies help to show what comes from genes as well as what is from a shared environment (twins share their environment) or a non-shared environment (twins have some environments they do not share, such as having different friends). Cross-cultural studies can help to show what in humans is from nature and genes and what is from nurture. The question of what comes from our nature and what comes from our nurture is called the '**nature-nurture debate**'. For example, if a procedure is repeated in different cultures and the same results are found, this suggests that what is being measured by the procedure is part of human nature. It has been said that attachment is one such characteristic. A characteristic found in all cultures (where it has been studied) and thought to be down to our nature is called a '**universal**' characteristic.

Questions & Answers

Issues and debates Role of nature and nurture in psychology Q1 focuses on what this means, and gives two examples to help to define it. Twin studies and obedience are the two examples offered.

Exam tip

You can offer evaluation of research to discuss the nature-nurture debate. For example, twin studies do not show 100% similarity in MZ twins, which suggests there is no characteristic that is purely 'nature'.

Knowledge check 35

Give one study that you have covered, apart from Milgram's studies, that considers gender differences in its results.

Exam tip

As with all the issues and debates in your course, be sure to have examples to use to show your understanding and to offer evaluation points. You can use Brendgen et al. (2005) as an example of a twin study (a contemporary study from biological psychology).

Knowledge check 36

If a characteristic is found in all cultures where it has been studied, this suggests it is a universal characteristic in humans (found in all humans) coming from human nature. What is another explanation for such a finding?

The development of psychology over time

Psychology has developed over time since the first laboratory was opened by Wundt in 1879. You need to be able to assess and evaluate the development of psychological understanding over time. You can do that by considering research in one area of study over time. If you looked at Burger (2009) as a contemporary study in social psychology you will know, for example, that Burger's replication of Milgram's work supported Milgram's claim that obedience is down to the situation.

In this example, psychological understanding over time developed to the extent of saying that the findings of Milgram still stood. Another example might be the multi-store model of memory which Baddeley took further when he developed the working memory model. These examples show how to build up enough material for this issue and debate.

> ### Exam tip
> When considering how psychological understanding has developed over time you could write a bit about research methods. For example, how access to and techniques about scanning have enabled more information (e.g. about the function of brain regions) to be uncovered, which has helped to build psychological understanding.

> ### Knowledge check 37
> Give an example from learning theories or biological psychology in your course where you can say that psychological understanding has developed over time.

The use of psychology in social control

Psychology is used in society as you found out when looking at key questions for society that can be informed by psychology. Psychology can also be used in **social control**. Social control refers to people being regulated by systems in a society, including their thoughts and feelings and also their behaviour. You have studied a lot of theories in psychology in your course and you will have seen that understanding in psychology can be used as a means of social control. Therapies and treatments are one example. For example, drug therapy controls individuals, such as limiting withdrawal symptoms and encouraging cessation of drug taking.

When you looked at learning theories you looked at treatments for phobias as well, such as systematic desensitisation, which could be seen as controlling people (e.g. overcoming their fear of flying). It is assumed that individuals wish to undertake such therapies, in which case they are perhaps in control rather than society, but you can see that there might be a case for saying that therapies and treatments are used as social control. This is the sort of discussion involved in this issue and debate.

> ### Exam tip
> You could use the key questions you have studied to see if they relate to social control. For example, controlling riots or reducing prejudice might be seen as society wishing to have control, and helping people with dementia might be about reducing the cost of care (however cynical that sounds).

> ### Knowledge check 38
> Give one example from your course where you saw psychology being used as a form of social control apart from therapies.

The use of psychological knowledge in society

For each of the topic areas in your course you covered at least one key question for society. When you used concepts, theories and/or research from a topic area to explain a key question for society you discussed the use of psychological knowledge in society. You can use your key questions to discuss this issue and debate and also bring in other material such as treatments and therapies, which use psychological knowledge in society.

Questions & Answers

Issues and debates Use of psychological knowledge in society Q1 focuses on two key questions from your course — how to prevent prejudice and the effectiveness of drug therapy.

Exam tip

You can use similar material for different questions (e.g. psychology used as social control is psychology used in society). Shape your answer to focus on the question — for example, if the question is about using psychology in society, you can look at how psychology can help to understand schizophrenia (not as control).

Issues related to socially sensitive research

The final issue and debate is an important one. You will have seen in your course how psychology often looks at issues that are sensitive in society. **Socially sensitive** research is research looking at issues that affect people and/or society in a negative way and issues that raise moral and ethical questions. Such issues can change over time. Currently socially sensitive research might be research looking at religious beliefs or, as has been the case for some time, research looking at racial aspects of people's behaviour.

Questions & Answers

Issues and debates Issues related to socially sensitive research Q1 asks for two examples to illustrate the definition offered. The two examples are Raine et al.'s (1997) study on 'murderers' and brain differences in them and Watson and Rayner (1920) and the use of conditioning to bring about a fear response or another response against someone's free will.

Exam tip

As with other issues and debates, when you are making notes, include examples from your course. You could use your textbook and go through the classic and contemporary studies as well as looking at the key questions you studied as you can use these as evidence.

Knowledge check 39

Explain one way in which psychological knowledge in clinical psychology has been useful in society.

Knowledge check 40

Explain one area of psychology that you have studied where research into the area is seen as 'socially sensitive'.

Summary: issues and debates

There are 11 issues and debates to cover in relation to your course. These are:

- ethical issues in research, including both research with animals and humans
- practical issues in the design and implementation of research
- reductionism in the explanation of behaviour
- comparisons of ways of explaining behaviour using different themes
- psychology as a science
- cultural and gender issues in psychological research
- the role of both nature and nurture in psychology
- an understanding of how psychological understanding has developed over time
- the use of psychology in social control
- the use of psychological knowledge in society
- issues related to socially sensitive research

Questions & Answers

Introduction

This section follows the basic structure of the psychological skills part of the course, with sample questions on methods first, then review of studies, then issues and debates. The questions themselves in this guide are not intended to represent the structure of Paper 3. Each of the three sections has questions to illustrate the sort of questions that can be asked but the marks do not add up to the marks for each section in the paper itself.

- **Methods** questions (Section A in Paper 3) range across the methods material throughout the course — 24 of the 80 marks on Paper 3 are for methods. There will be short questions and expect some longer questions worth up to 6 marks. This guide provides a range of questions to indicate the sorts of questions that can be asked.

- **Review of studies** (Section B in Paper 3) comprises 24 of the 80 marks and includes both extended writing and short-answer questions, like the ones included here. There can be an unseen study to focus on, as well as questions on studies you have covered in your course — the emphasis is on the classic studies.

- **Issues and debates** (Section C in Paper 3) is worth 32 of the 80 marks and comprises extended writing focusing on issues and debates, including a 20-mark essay. It is not possible to say exactly how the marks will appear in Section C in Paper 3, but, as an illustration, in the sample assessment materials (SAMs) found on the Edexcel website there is a 12-mark and a 20-mark question. Due to space constraints, this guide gives one 20-mark question and some short-answer questions. This is not what you would expect in the exam but will help you to practise.

Student Guides 1, 2 and 3 include issues and debates in their Question & Answer sections. Student Guide 1 considers 'practical issues in the design and implementation of research', Student Guide 2 looks at 'how psychology has changed over time' and Student Guide 3 covers 'psychology as science'. The sample assessment materials for your course also include a question on 'reductionism' in Paper 1 and a question on 'social control' in Paper 3. 'Ethics' are covered to an extent in this Question & Answer section in Section B Review of Studies: Unseen studies: understanding, evaluation and synopticity Q1c. Ethics are also covered in Student Guide 1, in the practical investigation for cognitive psychology, and in Student Guide 2, in the method question in learning theories. The five other issues and debates are the ones included here so you have access to a range of questions and answers on all the issues and debates to consider.

The sample questions can be used as practice questions for A-level Paper 3. The questions can also help with A-level Papers 1 and 2 in so far as they offer revision opportunities for material in those papers.

Examiner's comments

All questions and answers are followed by examiner's comments. These are preceded by the icon ⓔ or ⓔ. They indicate what a question requires, where credit is due, strengths in the answer, areas for improvement, specific problems, common errors, lack of clarity, irrelevance, mistakes in the meaning of terms and/or misinterpretation of the question. The comments also indicate how the answers might be marked in an exam — there are ticks in the answers to show where exactly marks are awarded.

Examination issues

Assessment objectives

You are marked according to assessment objectives (AOs). You can find these in the specification, but they are summarised here:

- **AO1** — knowledge with understanding of scientific ideas, processes, techniques and procedures (knowing and understanding)
- **AO2** — applying knowledge and understanding of scientific ideas, processes, techniques and procedures (applying)
- **AO3** — analysing, interpreting and evaluating a range of scientific information, ideas and evidence to make judgements and reach conclusions and also to refine practical design and procedures (commenting)

In Paper 3, approximately 25% of the marks are for AO1, 25% for AO2 and 50% for AO3, so you can see that you need to be prepared to analyse, interpret and evaluate.

Exam questions and marking

Your A-level exams will have some points-based marking and some levels-based marking:

- up to 8 marks is likely to mean points-based, which means 1 mark for each point clearly made
- 8 marks and over is likely to be levels marking, which means a mark depending on where in bands the answer fits — there are no ticks in these student answers

A-level Paper 3: In the methods section, quite a few questions are likely to be short-answer ones, focusing on one or more unseen studies, so that there is a focus on AO2 (applying your knowledge and understanding), as well AO3. In the review of studies and issues and debates sections, there are likely to be extended writing questions worth 8, 12, 16 or 20 marks. The questions with 8+ marks will use levels marking and the short-answer questions will use points-based marking. You can use what you learned about points-based and levels marking for Papers 1 and 2 to understand such marking for Paper 3.

Extended open-response questions: allocation of AOs

The different mark allocations for extended open-response questions have different assessment objective splits. This is worth knowing about. Extended open-response questions are from 8 marks onwards:

- 8 marks can be split into: AO1 4 marks and AO2* 4 marks; or AO1 4 marks and AO3 4 marks

- 12 marks can be split into: AO1 4 marks, AO2* 4 marks and AO3 4 marks; or AO1 6 marks and AO3 6 marks
- 16 marks can be split into: AO1 6 marks, AO2* 4 marks and AO3 6 marks; or AO1 6 marks and AO3 10 marks
- 20 marks can be split into: AO1 8 marks, AO2* 4 marks and AO3 8 marks; or AO1 8 marks and AO3 12 marks

*You will know if you need to focus on AO2 (applying your knowledge and understanding) because there will be a scenario of some sort to apply it to and a comment about you needing to refer to the scenario. Without a scenario to apply your knowledge and understanding to, the marks will be AO1 and AO3 with the splits as outlined here. AO2 always has 4 marks, as you can see.

Interpreting question command words

Questions have one command word, such as 'describe', 'assess' or 'calculate'. Appendix 6 in the specification lists the command words and what you have to do for each. Use the appendix to generate your own questions and make sure you do what is asked. For example, 'evaluate', 'assess', 'to what extent' and 'explain' all require you to come to a judgement in some way, or a conclusion.

How to use this section

- The questions in this section are sample Paper 3-type questions that can also help with Papers 1 and 2:
  - You can use the methods section to revise methods in the topic areas in your course.
  - You can use the review of studies section to help to revise the studies in the topic areas in your course.
  - You can use the issues and debates section to help with evaluation and comment in Papers 1 and 2.
- Choose each of the three sections in turn and revise the material using this Student Guide and your other books/notes. Work through the questions for your chosen section, answering them yourself without reading the advice on how to answer the question and without reading the answer given.
- Then read through the advice on what is required and mark your own answer. Did you interpret the question successfully? Read through the answers given and note where the marks were awarded. Finally, read through the comments to see what a full answer should include.
- Once you have prepared answers for all the questions in a particular area, answer them again, but this time choose a different focus/different material. For example, if you explained what the covert participant observation research method is, describe the overt non-participant observation research method. In this way you are making up your own questions, which is useful preparation for the examination — the '**Notes**' in the examiner's comments suggest ways you can do this.
- Specimen assessment materials can be found on the Edexcel website (www.edexcel.com), together with mark schemes. When you think you have revised enough, look them up and try to answer the questions. You may need your teacher to help you to access these materials.

■ Section A: Methods

Unseen study: a questionnaire

At a Canadian university 49 male and 87 female undergraduates completed a number of questionnaires all using a Likert scale. Some questionnaires focused on rating statements about their own humour styles (positive and negative, and also cheerfulness). Some focused on rating prejudice (including right-wing authoritarianism and social dominance orientation). The researchers wanted to see how individual differences in humour style and temperament (e.g. cheerfulness) related to prejudice. For example, people high in social dominance orientation, who could be seen as focusing on the dominance of one group over another, were thought to show aggressive humour styles, which related to hostility to an out-group. It was found that people higher in social dominance orientation reported more aggressive humour styles as was predicted, and there were other results as well, such as right-wing authoritarianism not correlating with humour styles, perhaps linking to being resistant to change.

The table below shows some correlations from the study — in this case between prejudiced personality, friendly humour style, cheerfulness and seriousness

Prejudiced personality	Aggressive humour style	Friendly humour style	Cheerful	Serious
Social dominance orientation	.34***	–.03	–.13	.06
Right wing authoritarianism	–.02	–.13	–.03	–.15

***$p<.001$

Adapted from Hodson et al. (2010)

(1) (a) In the findings given in the table, there is a reference to $p<.001$. Explain what $p<.001$ means. [3 marks]

ⓔ There are 3 points-based AO1 marks. There is 1 mark for each of the different elements of the notation and you do not have to give the context. The marks are AO1 because this is about knowing what $p<.001$ means rather than applying your understanding, which would be AO2. **Note:** you could check other such notations and explain what they mean, to change this question.

Student answer

'p' refers to level of significance, which is the chosen level at which a researcher would accept their alternate hypothesis. ✔ In this case the level of significance is said to be '<' which means 'less than' .001, which means 1 in 1000. ✔ This means the level of significance found is less than 1 in 1000 of the results being due to chance, which is an accepted level of significance — the findings would be seen as 'highly' significant. ✔

ⓔ **3/3 marks awarded.** There is clear understanding here of what all the elements of $p<.001$ mean and the whole answer is given as well — that this is a strong level of significance. You could add that 999 people out of 1000 would be expected to match the hypothesis, but there is enough here for the 3 marks.

(b) **Explain why the researchers used a correlation inferential test in this study.** (2 marks)

ⓔ There are 2 points-based AO2 marks. You need to relate your answer to the study so make sure you mention specifics. Recall what a correlation means and that should give you the answer. **Note:** you could write enough for 3 marks, or write about a different study that would use a different test, to change this question.

Student answer

The questionnaire used Likert-ranked data, which means scores were given to statements according to whether the individual 'strongly agreed' and so on. These are ordinal data. ✔ It was not claimed that humour style caused prejudice, just that there was possibly a relationship between a score about humour style and a score about prejudice, so what was looked for was a co-relationship. Thus a correlation test was required. ✔

ⓔ **2/2 marks awarded.** The two main elements of a correlation are that the data are ordinal and what is looked for is a relationship rather than a difference. The answer relates directly to the study, using the idea of Likert scales and attitudes like prejudice so the answer applies understanding, which is AO2 and is what is asked for. For a third mark, if there was one, you could have brought in the suggestion that a Spearman's test would suit or you could explain more about how humour and prejudice might come from one cause so might be related but not one causing the other. However, this question just has the 2 marks.

(c) **Discuss how far the study given here can be used as evidence for the social identity theory explanation of prejudice as coming from hostility to an out-group. You must make reference to the context in your answer.** (8 marks)

ⓔ There are 8 levels-based marks. With 8 marks if there is a requirement to link to a context as there is here, the split is 4 AO1 and 4 AO2. When you see the phrase 'you must make reference to the context in your answer' you know you have to answer in the context of the question, in this case the study. 'Discuss' requires you to give different viewpoints and ideas, so you need to give ideas about the study supporting the theory and other views too, perhaps how the theory is not supported. **Note:** you could consider looking at a different theory or construct relating to this study, such as right-wing authoritarianism, to change this question.

Questions & Answers

Student answer

Social identity theory puts forward the ideas of in-group favouritism and out-group hostility and the study suggests that people showing social dominance orientation (SDO) are likely to see their group as dominant over another group, which is an in-group/out-group suggestion **[AO1]**. Therefore, those with social dominance orientation are prejudiced through showing hostility to the out-group and in the study should show more aggression and less friendship towards the out-group.

The study found that there was a significant positive correlation between social dominance orientation and aggressive humour, which backs the social identity theory, showing hostility to the out-group. The finding was at the level of $p<.001$, which is a strong finding **[AO1]**, so the evidence is rather strong. However, questionnaires use self-report data and there might have been social desirability in that participants answered how they thought they should answer **[AO1]**, which means the data might not show validity.

It is interesting that the data shown suggest the only significant relationship was between SDO and aggressive humour, which possibly is evidence for the theory since other ideas were not evidenced. However, it was thought that right-wing authoritarianism, suggesting someone would not like change **[AO1]**, would not relate to any of the humour/cheerfulness and this was found (since results showed no significant correlation) so there was perhaps more to the findings of the study than just supporting social identity theory.

e **4/8 marks awarded.** Q9 in Paper 2 in the Edexcel sample assessment materials (page 111) shows a levels-based mark scheme you can use for this question. The highest level requires accurate and thorough knowledge and understanding. 'AO1' in brackets after a point indicates that there is some AO1 content in that point. This answer does give some accurate knowledge and understanding, but quite a lot of this comes from the source and it is not 'thorough' so this answer is not in the top level for AO1.

With regard to AO2, there is a grasp of some competing arguments, such as a criticism of questionnaire data and a considering of the RWA finding and some logical chains of reasoning, using scientific ideas, processes, techniques and procedures (e.g. social desirability and levels of significance). The answer is somewhat superficial, however, and you would expect to write more than this for 8 marks. This answer is somewhere between Level 2 and Level 3, possibly 4 out of 8 marks.

Unseen study: a laboratory experiment

Thirty participants agreed to take part in an experiment. Individually they each read a passage about land use. All participants read the same passage. However, in one condition the passage was said to be written by a land agent representing investors wanting to develop the land and in the other condition the passage was said to be written by an environmentalist representing people opposed to the development of the land. The participants were randomly split into the two conditions. After the participants had read the passage including the information about the writer of the passage, the experimenter read out some recognition items. These were sentences associated with the passage. The participants had to write 'yes' or 'no' according to whether they thought each sentence was actually in the passage they had read. Two sentences were straight from the passage (participants should say 'yes') and two sentences gave likely information but were not actually in the passage (participants should say 'no').

Then there were 10 other sentences altered to suit the view held by the person supposed to have written the passage and importantly all 10 sentences were not in the passage. Five of the 'false' 10 sentences favoured the environmentalist (e.g. 'development of the land would negatively affect wildlife in the area') and five favoured the land agent (e.g. 'development of the land would bring much-needed jobs to the area'). The question was would the participants falsely recognise sentences that suited the view of the person they had been told had written the passage? If false recognition was found, this suggests that memory is affected by perception of the writer's intention and memory is not exact, like a tape recorder. The researchers thought that there would be more false recognition of the sentences that 'suited' what the participants might see as the intention of the writer of the passage.

The table shows the results of the experiment: scores are the mean number of false sentences (out of 5) where the participant says 'yes', the sentence is in the passage.

	Mean number of false sentences agreed to be in the passage: land agent focused	Mean number of false sentences agreed to be in the passage: environmentalist focused
Land agent 'wrote' the passage	3.07	1.73
Environmentalist 'wrote' the passage	1.93	3.93

Adapted from Wertsch (1974)

(1) (a) State what experimental design is used in the experiment. (1 mark)

ⓔ There is 1 points-based mark for the design. 'State' means 'give' and as the designs are 'named' you should give the term itself. **Note:** you could use the same question for other experiments you can make up as 'unseen' ones or find using an internet search, to change this question.

Questions & Answers

ⓔ **1/1 mark awarded.** There are three experimental designs — repeated measures, independent groups and matched pairs. This one just says that participants are randomly allocated to one of two conditions so it is an independent groups design. It is not mentioned that participants were matched, so we assume they were not.

(b) Explain one way that the researchers may have randomly split the participants into the two groups.

(2 marks)

ⓔ There are 2 points-based marks — one for giving a 'way' and one for justification of the answer, which is what 'explain' requires. **Note:** you could use the same question and generate another answer, or answer a question such as 'why is random allocation to groups used?' to change this question.

Student answer

There were just 30 participants so all their names could go into a box and as a name was pulled out the participant could be put into Condition One, the next into Condition Two and then Condition One and so on until they are all allocated to one or the other condition. ✔✔

ⓔ **2/2 marks awarded.** This would lead to randomisation because each participant has an equal chance of being in either condition. There should be no bias regarding age, gender or any other participant characteristics as all the names are there to be picked out each time.

(c) Explain whether the results of the experiment supported the experimental hypothesis or not.

(3 marks)

ⓔ There are 3 points-based AO2 marks. You need to make it clear that you have understood the experimental hypothesis and then use the results in the table to explain what was found. Then relate the findings to the hypothesis. **Note:** you could generate other questions about this experiment, such as what inferential test could be used, to change this question.

Student answer

The hypothesis is that participants would falsely remember statements in the passage more if they focused on the point of view of the person purporting to have written the passage than if they were from a different viewpoint. When the viewpoint and the writer matched (e.g. land agent was the 'writer' and the view was in favour of the land being developed), both for the land agent and the environmentalist the mean was a lot higher (3.07 and 3.93 average agreement with the sentence out of 5) than if there was no match (1.73 and 1.93). ✔✔ This means that the experimental hypothesis was indeed supported by the findings and there was more agreement with sentences being in the passage (falsely) if the sentence viewpoint matched the 'writer' than if it did not. ✔

ⓔ **3/3 marks awarded.** The relationship of the hypothesis to the results is clear and all four figures are used to show the relationship, so a double tick is given after all that information. It is not that there is a mark for the hypothesis, as that was not in the question, but part of the double mark is for accurately understanding the hypothesis in relation to the figures found. The final sentence makes it clear what the answer is — the hypothesis is supported — so gets the final mark. You could see this answer as having that final sentence first, as the answer, and then the rest of the material being the justification (so suiting the injunction 'explain').

Unseen study: an animal laboratory experiment

The experiment used 48 male rats to see if having multiple items in their cage enriched rats compared with having single items. There were four rats in each cage. The different conditions/treatments included cages with 'crawl balls' that rats could crawl into and roll, ladder cages they could climb up, cages with wooden blocks in them, retreat cages, cages with chew bones, and cages with all of the options, called 'multiple item' cages.

The behaviour of the rats was observed every week in two sessions on one day for each of the conditions/treatments. The observation lasted 5 weeks. There were 10 second intervals between recording the behaviour of an animal in an observation period. There were eight behaviours noted per rat and this was done in two sessions on one day for each rat, so 16 behaviours noted each week. Over 5 weeks this meant there were 80 behaviours noted over the course of the experiment.

The researchers tested each rat's behaviour in the two sessions as a comparison and they did this over the 5 weeks to see if the two weekly observations of each rat matched, to test for reliability. The researchers tested the behaviour between the conditions/treatments for each rat as well, to see if those with multiple items in their cage (four rats) were more enriched by the stimulation. Researchers also measured weight gain and organ weights of all the rats in the study.

Results showed that sleep, contact and enrichment-directed behaviour was shown more by the rats where there were multiple items in the cage.

Adapted from Abou-Ismail (2011)

(1) (a) How many conditions/treatments were there in the study? (1 mark)

ⓔ There is 1 points-based AO2 mark. This is a question to check your understanding and is AO2 because it is about the study. **Note:** you could generate other questions about this experiment, such as where there is an example of time sampling or why time sampling might be used, to change this question.

> **Student answer**
>
> Six. ✔

@ **1/1 mark awarded.** Six conditions is correct. There is the 'crawl ball' condition, the ladder cage condition, wooden blocks is a third condition, retreat cages is a fourth condition, chew bones a fifth and the important 'multiple items' is the sixth condition.

(b) Explain how in the study there is one example of a repeated measures design and one of an independent groups design. (4 marks)

@ There are 4 points-based AO2 marks. This is a question to check your understanding and it is AO2 because it is about the study. The researchers analyse the study in terms of repeated measures and also use an independent groups design. There will be 2 marks for each of these: 1 mark for a brief answer and 1 mark for justifying the answer. **Note:** you could generate other questions about the design of this experiment, such as strengths or weaknesses of the two designs in relation to how they were used in this study, to change this question.

Student answer

When researchers compare their observations of the same rat over the two sessions that make up the observation for that week, they are using a repeated measures design because the behaviours from the same rat at more or less the same time are being compared. ✔✔ When the researchers are comparing the behaviour of the rats in the six different conditions, and comparing 'between' the conditions, that is an independent groups design. ✔

@ **3/4 marks awarded.** This answer is fairly thorough. The part about repeated measures is clear and shows good understanding of what repeated measures means as well as how it is found in this study, so both marks are given. However, the part about the independent groups design, though accurate, does not quite say that the behaviours between the rats in the six conditions will mean different rats in each condition so just 1 mark is given. This answer comes very close to getting all 4 marks — this emphasises the need to make a thorough and detailed point for each mark.

(c) Explain one practical issue when using animals in laboratory experiments in psychology to find out about human behaviour. (2 marks)

@ There are 2 points-based AO3 marks. This question is AO3 because it is about a problem (or a strength) of using animals. Answer using a practical issue not an ethical one. You are not asked about this particular study so you can focus in general on using animals in laboratory experiments. There is 1 mark for the issue and 1 mark for elaboration. **Note:** you could find two practical issues, or look at ethical issues/problems, to change this question.

Student answer

A practical issue with using animals in laboratory experiments when wanting to find out about human behaviour is in setting up a situation that is sufficiently valid to apply to humans. ✔ For example, in this study enrichment was provided by using multiple items in a cage with four rats sharing a cage and the items. This might not represent an enriched environment for humans. For example, it might be just that there are more items in the 'multiple item' cage and this might not represent more enrichment, just more items. ✔

ⓔ **2/2 marks awarded.** The answer chooses one practical issue — how to represent human behaviour in a laboratory experiment involving animals. That gets 1 mark. Then the elaboration was needed. The answer uses the study as an example to show the problem with validity, which is fine. Just because you do not have to relate your answer to the context does not mean you cannot do that, as long as the elaboration helps to justify the issue you choose to raise. The issue is elaborated here and the second mark is given.

(d) With reference to this study, explain one way in which the study could have been improved.

(2 marks)

ⓔ There are 2 points-based AO3 marks. This question is AO3 because it is about improving a study — you should expect questions asking for improvements. This question is very broad. In an exam it might be related to the practical issue in the question before it (though that would then have to ask about a 'practical problem'). Here it is not linked. Any relevant improvement would gain marks. There is 1 mark for the improvement and 1 mark for justification of the suggestion. **Note:** you could consider two improvements or a question linked to the 'practical issue' you gave, to change this question.

Student answer

One improvement could be to have the same number of items in each condition. This would mean giving 5 wooden blocks, 5 ladders, 5 chew bones and 5 crawl balls (though perhaps 'retreat space' is okay) in those different conditions. Then the 'multiple items' condition has 1 wooden block, 1 ladder, 1 chew bone, 1 crawl ball and a retreat space. ✔ This is so that it was not just 'multiple items' that was the main condition but 'multiple items giving different enrichment possibilities'.✔

ⓔ **2/2 marks awarded.** The improvement is in trying to control for the presence of 'many items' needing to be controlled for and the answer elaborates on why this is important. It is important not to rely on the answer before, which is about the practical issue, as the questions are not linked and the examiner will see just this question and answer. There is enough elaboration to get the second mark in this answer, though the explanation of how the hypothesis was about 'multiple enrichment possibilities' rather than just 'multiple items' is a bit brief.

Qualitative data

A study was done using analysis of keywords to compare the characteristics of research interviews with postings to online forums. The aim was to look at the usefulness of these two methods to find out about the experience of illness. There are advantages of using the internet to gather data, such as the inclusion of people not in the geographic area of an interview study, and also large amounts of data can be collected in a short space of time. Data can be anonymous too, and people might give data they might not give to an interviewer. In the study, 140 interviews were carried out with people with health problems and data were compared with data posted on two online forums focusing on two health problems — breast cancer and prostate cancer.

It was possible to get full informed consent from participants about being interviewed, but this was not possible with regard to the forums data.

It was found that interviewing gathered information about past events and what they meant to the interviewee, whereas internet forums focused more on current illness experiences. In the interviews, the interviewer guided the data gathered and the presence of the interviewer seemed to mean the interviewee put forward a view of an 'acceptable' self. Although in an interview there can be probing and richer more detailed data are uncovered compared to forum data. Forum postings are not so much someone telling their story, but are about getting emotional support and information. There is more detail about an illness itself in the forum postings, for example. A difficulty for researchers is that they have not helped to collect forum data so the data might not fully answer a research question.

Adapted from Seale et al. (2009)

(1) (a) Explain two advantages the study found regarding using forum data rather than interview data.

(4 marks)

(e) There are 2 points-based AO2 marks. The question asks you to pick out two advantages mentioned in the study with regard to the forum data. 'Explain' means give the advantage you find in the study and then explain it as an advantage to justify your answer. You need to do this for two advantages. **Note:** you could look for advantages of the interviewing, or disadvantages, to change the question.

> **Student answer**
>
> One advantage of the forum data is that they focus on current information about experiences more than interviewing does and the data are less of a story about what had happened. ✔ They also give more detail about some features of their experiences such as about the actual illness. ✔ Interviews are better for probing into certain areas and the researcher has more opportunity to make sure they have the data they need to answer their research question.

ⓔ 2/4 marks awarded. Overall, this answer is not well focused on the question, though it does give two advantages of using forum data rather than interview data. One advantage is the focus on current information and not retrospective information, and the other is the focus on detail about the illness. The second advantage is not very clear. Adding that the interview seemed to get the 'acceptable' self instead would have added to it. Neither of the advantages is expanded on so they are both 'stated' rather than 'explained' so 1 mark only for each. There are also two advantages of using interviewing, but that is not what the question asks for. The first advantage given about forum data could be developed by adding a point about validity as current experiences are likely to be more valid than thinking back on how the person felt. The second advantage could also be about validity, adding that the forum data seemed to be more about what the person wanted to say about their experiences of the illness than about what the interviewer wanted to find out. The answer needed to be about the findings of the study not about advantages of internet data in general. Make sure you answer the question explicitly.

(b) Explain the advantages of using qualitative data over quantitative data, including one example from this study. (4 marks)

ⓔ There are 4 points-based marks: 1 AO2 mark for including an example from the study and 3 AO3 marks for explaining advantages. 'Advantages' is plural so give more than one. **Note:** you could use disadvantages instead of advantages, or consider ethical problems in this study, to change this question.

Student answer

Qualitative data give a richness and detail that quantitative data do not produce. In a study about someone's experiences it is the richness and personal feelings that are wanted and not answers to closed questions such as how bad they feel on a scale of 1 to 7 and so qualitative data are sought. ✔ An example from the study is where on a forum someone will give more detail about their illness than if they are interviewed, and they use the forum for emotional support as well as information. Such information, detail and support need to be in the form of qualitative data, which is an advantage of such data. ✔ (AO2) A specific advantage of qualitative data over quantitative data is that the individual gives information they choose to give, which is a focus for them, and so will be valid in terms of being about their experiences and emotions. ✔ Quantitative data are answers to questions chosen by researchers to suit what the researcher wants to know rather than to let the respondent guide the data. This means validity is threatened. ✔

ⓔ 4/4 marks awarded. There is a lot of material in this answer. The example is well-outlined and suits the answer so the AO2 mark is given. Then there are 3 marks for the AO3 content. In general it takes longer to get an AO3 mark than an AO1 or AO2 mark because in it takes longer for an evaluation point to be made, so bear in mind you need to make points clearly. Also the injunction is to explain, which means make a point and justify it. You can see in this answer that there is not just a focus on good things about qualitative data, the answer also shows how qualitative data are 'better then' quantitative data in the ways suggested, which is what the question asks for, and the last mark is given for elaboration.

■ Section B: Review of studies

Classic studies

You will have covered one classic study in clinical psychology and one in your other application from criminological, child and health psychology.

Application	Classic study
Clinical	Rosenhan (1973)
Criminological	Loftus and Palmer (1974)
Child	Van IJzendoorn and Kroonenberg (1988)
Health	Olds and Milner (1959)

(1) (a) Evaluate the procedure of Rosenhan (1973) compared with the procedure of the classic study in the other application you studied. (8 marks)

ⓔ There are 8 levels-based marks: 4 AO1 marks and 4 AO3 marks. There is no requirement for you to relate your answer to a context so there are no AO2 marks. You need to focus on the procedure of Rosenhan (1973) and the procedure of your other classic study. Here Loftus and Palmer (1974) is chosen as an example. The AO1 marks should come from your evaluation as you will show knowledge and understanding as you evaluate. Concentrate mostly on similarities, differences, advantages and disadvantages, always focusing on the procedure of each study. **Note:** you could substitute 'procedure' with 'ethics', 'results', 'hypotheses', 'sampling and participants' to change the question. Or you could choose two different classic studies without focus on the applications in your course, such as Raine et al. (1997) and Watson and Rayner (1920) and keep the wording of the question the same, to change the question.

Student answer

Rosenhan used eight participants, including himself, to individually visit 12 hospitals presenting with hearing 'thud' or something similar in the head, but otherwise giving their 'real' background and information **[AO1]**. Loftus and Palmer (1974) used students and showed them films of car accidents then asked them various questions about the accidents including the speed of the car in the film **[AO1]**. Loftus and Palmer used a laboratory experiment method. Rosenhan's study used 12 case studies of individuals and how they got on after presenting themselves at the hospital **[AO1]**. Rosenhan gathered mainly qualitative data such as notes about how the pseudo-patient was treated whereas Loftus and Palmer used quantitative data in the form of the estimated speed in miles per hour and 'yes' or 'no' to whether there was broken glass **[AO1]**. Rosenhan's aim was to look at the validity of the diagnosis of mental health disorders so he needed depth and detail in his data to see how the pseudo-patients were treated, which led to him wanting qualitative data **[AO1]**. However, Loftus and Palmer's procedure focused on reliability as they wanted to see how a word affected witness testimony rather than detail about someone's experiences, which is why they chose the experimental method **[AO1]**.

It was the difference in research question that led to a different choice of research method and different procedures — case studies are good for depth, detail and richness, while experiments are good for replicability and objectivity. Rosenhan's procedure just involved eight participants, but there were 12 hospitals and so some generalisability, whereas Loftus and Palmer, though they used more students, only chose students, which limited the generalisability, possibly. One issue is that using students in psychology studies might limit what is found because just a 'student' view is found out about. Rosenhan controlled how the participants presented themselves to the hospital by asking them all to say they heard something in their head, but he then left it up to the pseudo-patient, whereas Loftus and Palmer used more controls, such as all seeing the same films and having all the same questions except for the one word change that was the independent variable. This makes Loftus and Palmer's study more scientific and objective, able to claim cause-and-effect conclusions, though as said above it does raise doubts about validity. In conclusion, it can be seen that the two procedures are very different, with one focusing on qualitative data and validity, and the other emphasising reliability, quantitative data, objectivity, science and cause-and-effect conclusions.

ℯ 5/8 or 6/8 marks awarded. Page 32 of the sample assessment materials that you can find on the Edexcel website gives a suitable levels mark scheme for this question. The AO1 points are noted to an extent in this answer, though there is AO1 that is not noted here as well because it is embedded in the answer, such as showing understanding of terms like 'generalisability'. There is a lot of AO1 but not enough to call it 'thorough' so it does not reach Level 4. With regard to the evaluation of the procedures and comparing them, there are some good evaluation points around reliability, validity, type of data, objectivity, generalisability and 'doing science'. The terms are used well. The conclusion is not bad but does not mention generalisability. The structure is good with some AO1 points given first followed by some evaluation points. Overall, there is some useful material here but not enough for Level 4, so Level 3 seems a suitable level for this answer. Notice that the comparison points made in the first half of the answer are still AO1 as they are not directly evaluating the two procedures.

(b) Explain two points from one of the classic studies you covered that help to show why it is a 'classic' study and so a valuable study to learn. (4 marks)

ℯ There are 4 points-based marks: 2 AO1 marks for knowledge and understanding of the study and 2 AO3 marks for evaluation points focusing on why the study is 'classic', though more than two points about the study being 'classic' could be made. This question is points-based and short answer, whereas you should practise extended writing questions for this section. However, it helps to show the sorts of questions that can be asked and how you might answer them. You are not likely to have prepared for every possible question so practise using your learning to answer questions you might not have expected (perhaps like this one). Watson and Rayner's (1920) study is chosen here. 'Explain' needs two points to be made and then both elaborated and justified. **Note:** you could answer the same question for all your 'classic studies' to change the question.

Student answer

Watson and Rayner's (1920) Little Albert study was done a long time ago and is still being covered in psychology courses. It must be 'classic' and important to still be studied [point 1]. In that period a lot of learning theory studies used animals, such as Skinner using pigeons and Pavlov using dogs. Watson and Rayner used a human baby, so that made the study of great interest ✔ [point 2, includes some AO1]. Another reason for it having such importance is that it highlighted how fear can be learned and focused on children learning such fears, so there is a practical application to the study in terms of how children are brought up ✔ [point 3, includes some AO1]. When a study has a strong practical application and is methodologically strong and interesting, that contributes to its 'classic' status ✔ [points 2 and 3 elaborated on a little, some AO3], as well perhaps as when it is done by someone well-known in the field, as Watson was [point 4]. Another reason might be the publication of the study, which involved a film as well as research papers so the study was well-disseminated and known about [point 5, includes some AO1].

ⓔ **3/4 marks awarded.** The 2 AO1 marks are clearly here — five points are picked out. The other 2 marks are for AO3 which means they should be justified, which is what is missing from this answer. There is some elaboration of points two and three, which has been given 1 AO3 mark, but the other justification mark has not been awarded. This answer would work better for a more general question — when 'points' are asked for, as is done here, your focus has to be precise.

Classic studies: issues and debates

1   Choose two classic studies from the topics you have studied in your course and assess how far they show that psychology understanding has developed over time.

(12 marks)

ⓔ There are 12 marks broken down into 6 AO1 marks and 6 AO3 marks. You do not have to relate to any context, so there are no AO2 marks for this question. For 8- and 12-mark questions, with no AO2, there is an even split of AO1 and AO3 marks. You need to focus on two classic studies and how they show the development of psychological understanding, and then assess how far this is the case, coming to a judgement. This can include how far they do not show the development of understanding, or how others have done that better.

It is worth taking a short while to choose which two studies you will use. Think of two that perhaps do show how psychology has developed, or one that does and one that clearly does not. As these are classic studies they are likely to show development, though they can be classic because of their uniqueness. **Note:** you could answer this question a few times, using different studies, or using a different issue and debate, or giving more marks, to change the question.

Student answer

One classic study is Rosenhan (1973) and the focus is on testing the validity of mental health diagnosis. This is a novel method and a novel focus which did not build on previous understanding, but it did develop psychological understanding. The issue is that Rosenhan's study did not show the development of psychological understanding building on other studies, it was exploratory.

However, Baddeley (1966b) did show development of psychological understanding over time, though not over a long period. He built on studies he had done himself and also on theory. The main theory was the multi-store model of memory, showing two main parts of memory, short-term and long-term memory. Baddeley (1966b) knew from other work that short-term memory used an acoustic store so words that sounded alike would affect the learning of a list in short-term memory more than words that had similar meaning. He wanted to know whether long-term memory also used acoustic processing. He used 'sound-alike' words and words with similar meaning. He found that long-term memory used semantic processing, unlike short-term memory and this added to the evidence for there being two different stores, as the multi-store model had suggested. In fact, Baddeley went on to look more at short-term memory and proposed his working memory model (with Hitch) not long afterwards, in 1974. This looked at acoustic coding and suggested there is an articulatory loop to help to review the memory trace and a phonological store which stores the sound. The phonological store is the 'inner ear' and the articulatory loop is the 'inner voice' repeating sounds to rehearse them. The working memory model, which became an alternative to the multi-store model, was developed by Baddeley over time. In 2000, for example, he added the episodic buffer to the idea of the phonological store and visuospatial sketchpad.

Baddeley (1966b) in his procedure used an interference task which he would know about from ideas from Brown (1958) and Peterson (1959), which became known as the Brown-Peterson technique, again showing how studies build on one another to build a body of psychological knowledge and psychological understanding develops over time. Peterson et al. (2002) looked at interference in a well-known test in psychology using fMRI, which shows how understanding continues to develop over time. Interference in fact started to be studied and understood as far back as 1924 with a study by Jenkins and Dallenbach showing how what happens during the day can interfere with memory.

From the two classic studies used here, it seems that some psychological studies do build on psychological understanding and over time develop ideas and theories, just as Baddeley (1966b) built on his and the work of others and then went on to develop a different model of memory. Studies like this are explanatory, looking to explain some aspect of human behaviour or processing. Similarly the idea of interference as a theory of forgetting was built on. However, other studies, such as Rosenhan (1973) are exploratory, which means they are not building on the work of others, they have a more novel research question and use novel means of uncovering data to suit their question. Often exploratory studies gather qualitative data whereas explanatory studies use quantitative data and a more scientific approach.

(e) **8/12 or 9/12 marks awarded.** Page 97 of the A-level sample assessment materials gives a levels mark scheme for 8-mark 'Assess' questions. One for 12 marks would require similar features in the answer, but more marks would be available. For the top level you would need to give 'accurate and thorough knowledge and understanding' and with regard to AO3, a 'well-developed and logical assessment' with an 'awareness of the significance of competing arguments' leading to a 'balanced judgement'. That is what is being looked for here.

This answer is accurate and thorough regarding Baddeley's study but much less detailed regarding Rosenhan's study. There is a lot of detail about how Baddeley's study builds psychological understanding over time, including the focus on 'time', and the AO1 is in the top level. However, the other study is much less detailed. Having said that, Rosenhan's study was a good choice because it offers an argument about differences in the focus of studies depending on their research question, which addresses the 'assess' injunction well. Also, there was not as much to say about Rosenhan's study precisely because it did not really build on previous studies as Baddeley's did, and the amount of detail that is possible must be taken into account. The argument about studies being explanatory or exploratory is good. You might not have known these terms, but you could give the points without the terms and that would be okay.

There is a lot of focus in this answer on the 'issue and debate' which is what the question requires, drawing on two classic studies. Overall, it is a good answer, but perhaps needs a bit more detail about Rosenhan, so does not quite reach the top level.

Unseen studies

A study looked at cameras placed as a deterrent where there were red traffic lights. It wanted to see whether the strategy of the camera always working was better than the strategy of moving the 'working' camera around to different red lights so that motorists did not know whether a specific camera was operational or not. If a driver thinks a camera will not be 'on' they may think there is no punishment for them 'jumping' the red light. The study looked at a system of randomly allocating which camera was 'on' (a variable schedule), a system for using a set cycle for which camera was 'on' (a fixed schedule) and a system with no rotation (a continuous schedule). It was thought that the continuous schedule would be the most effective, because each time a driver approached the red light, they would see there would be punishment for 'jumping' the light compared with the other two schedules where there might not be punishment. From an economic viewpoint having all the cameras on might not be useful, so the researchers also looked at the other two options and thought the fixed schedule of cycling the cameras would be more efficient than the variable schedule, but that there would not be much difference. The researchers in cooperation with the police set things up using some cameras in a busy city so that the different schedules were in operation and could be recorded along with the traffic levels and the violation rates. The normal system in the city was to move the limited number of cameras around to different locations.

The table shows the violation rates (jumping the red light) for the different schemes. The rate is the percentage of the traffic.

Scheme	Mean %	Standard deviation
Fixed/continuous	0.0211	0.0014
Cyclical/fixed interval	0.0836	0.0767
Random/variable interval	0.0770	0.0432

An important conclusion was that punishment is better when it is predictable and likely to happen, which is in contrast with systems of rewards, which seem to be better if unpredictable even though likely to happen at some stage. The researchers concluded that it is more effective to keep the cameras that are available fixed at the most dangerous locations than to spread them around locations either in rotation or randomly.

Adapted from Tay and de Barros (2011)

1 (a) Using the results in the table explain the results of the study. (3 marks)

ⓔ There are 3 points-based AO2 marks. The marks would be for using the actual numbers in the table to show the results — 1 mark for each clear result point given. You could consider using the standard deviation scores. If asked to use data from a table, try to use as much of the information as possible. This question tests understanding. **Note:** you could answer the same question for other studies you have covered, or find other unseen studies if possible, to change the question.

Student answer

There is a clear difference in the percentage of violations between the fixed condition where the camera was always on and the other two conditions, where the camera was not always on, but was either randomly on or on according to a set cycle. The figure is 0.0211 compared with the two other figures which were 0.0836 and 0.0770. ✔ There is a strong similarity in the percentage violation rates when the camera is not always on, which is when it is randomly or cyclically on. The figures are 0.0836 and 0.0770 which are rather similar compared with the 'always on' condition. ✔ Standard deviation differs in that it is very small (0.0014) in the 'continuously on' condition, larger in the 'cyclical' condition (0.0767) and somewhere between the two figures for the 'random' condition (0.0432). The spread of scores, therefore, is very small in the 'fixed' condition which suggests motorists in the main did not 'run' the red light in that condition. ✔

ⓔ **3/3 marks awarded.** A lot of information is given for each mark as a main point is made and then the figures given to support it. You might think that for 'explain', the point and then the figures would get 1 mark each, but it is best to work on marks not being given so quickly in Paper 3, which is the synoptic paper and looking for depth in the understanding.

(b) Most researchers will draw on theory to underpin their study and to help when drawing conclusions. Explain the study given here using one theory you have studied in your course.

(4 marks)

ⓔ There are 4 points-based AO2 marks. You would expect the source to guide you towards a certain topic area, so look for that and then from that recall the theories and see if you can apply one of them. This question tests synopticity as it requires you to draw on theory from your course to explain a study. **Note:** you could see if you can find two or more theories, or look for another study using the internet and apply this question to that study, to change the question.

Student answer

The researchers mention punishment and rewards, which suggests that operant conditioning is being used as a theory to guide the study. Skinner put forward the idea of behaviour being learned by reinforcement schedules such that rewards each time were less effective than a variable interval schedule of rewards. ✔ This means that someone would know there would be a reward but would not know when the reward would come. Skinner found that continuous reinforcement was not as effective as variable reinforcement and rewarding at fixed intervals was less effective than a variable schedule too.

ⓔ **1/4 marks awarded.** The theory is right — the researchers did draw on operant conditioning though the summary of the study here does not say so. It is good to use the name of the person involved and the name of the theory, and a bit more in the first two sentences might have earned 2 marks instead of just 1 mark. Perhaps the student could have added more about positive and negative reinforcement and punishment, or about it being a theory of learning that can apply to all behaviour including 'jumping' red lights. The mark is given when a bit more detail is added, about variable interval schedules being best according to Skinner, which is an important part of the theory for this study. However, the rest of the material does not say much more and is not quite enough for another mark. Also, the answer must relate to the source. Saying that the study found when focusing on punishment the opposite from Skinner's findings about rewards would help to focus the answer and gain another mark. A conclusion adding to the theory would also add a mark, suggesting that when it comes to punishment it needs to be predictable to be effective, which seems not to be the case regarding rewards.

(c) Explain one strength and one weakness of the study given here.

(6 marks)

ⓔ There are 6 points-based marks. There could be 2 AO2 marks because you have to unpick the study to find one strength and one weakness, and 4 AO3 marks — 2 for the strength and 2 for the weakness, because you are using your evaluation skills. This question focuses on evaluation. **Note:** you could change the question to look at two strengths or two weaknesses, to change the question.

Student answer

One weakness in this study relates to its ethics. For example, changes to how cameras are used to deter 'jumping a red light' behaviour thereby changing whether a camera is in use or not might affect driving behaviour, leading to an accident, which would be causing harm, an ethical principle in psychology that goes with responsibility according to the BPS Code of Ethics and Conduct (2009). ✔ However, the police department was involved and agreed with the ideas about which cameras were 'on' and which were not 'on'. Also this was the strategy at the time in any case so the study did not instigate the idea of cameras not being 'on'. ✔ Another issue regarding the ethics weakness was that drivers were not involved in the study in that they did not give consent. A driver 'caught' by one of the cameras used in the study was punished for the violation. However, it could be argued that the driver should not be jumping a red light and cameras were likely to be on, so the researchers did not cause any difference really. ✔ A strength was in the validity of the findings. The study addressed a real-life problem and though whether a camera was a real one or not was manipulated, this was what happened in the city in any case, ✔ so though there was a clear independent variable it was manipulated in the field and there was clear ecological validity. This means that conclusions from the study could be applied as the findings were valid. ✔

ⓔ **5/6 marks awarded.** The weakness is ethics — this is taken as one weakness even though two issues are raised. They are both about 'not causing harm' so can be taken as one weakness and it is clearly stated that 'ethics' is the weakness so giving two examples was accepted. The AO1 point is clear and brings in BPS guidelines which adds some depth and there are two more points which relate the 'doing no harm' and 'not getting consent' ethical points (the AO1) to the source (AO2). The strength does not have enough for 3 marks, but there is enough for 2 marks. The AO1 part about validity in that the IV was manipulated but in the field is clear enough and the relating to the study is also clear. However, there is not enough for a third mark. Perhaps adding more about how participants were involved in their normal behaviour and had a choice about their driving behaviour (whether to jump the red light or not) gave the study validity would earn the third mark.

■ Section C: Issues and debates

Comparisons of ways of explaining behaviour using different themes

(1) Psychology studies the behaviour of people with mental disorders. Focusing on one mental disorder, explain one strength and one weakness in the way two different themes explain the behaviour of people with that mental disorder. (6 marks)

ⓔ There are 6 points-based marks: 2 AO1 marks and 4 AO3 marks. This question illustrates the sort of question that might arise, but in issues and debates you would expect levels marked questions. Here you are asked to show knowledge and understanding of two different themes that explain the behaviour of people with a particular mental disorder. Choose one of the disorders you have studied, think of two different explanations (using different themes) and then give one strength and one weakness of each of the explanations. **Note:** you could then answer the question again using your other disorder, and/or changing your two chosen themes, to change the question. You could also remove the 'one' relating to both the strength and the weakness and use the terms 'strengths' and 'weaknesses' and make this a 20-mark essay.

Student answer

Schizophrenia can be explained using different themes. Two clearly different themes are looking at biology or looking at social factors to explain the behaviour of people with schizophrenia. One biological explanation is neurotransmitter functioning and excess dopamine is said to be a reason for the behaviour of people with schizophrenia, such as hallucinations and disordered thinking. ✔Social factors such as lack of social support can affect the behaviour of people with schizophrenia, and it is shown that having social support can help **[some of the information about connectedness, given later, is added to this sentence to make this a full tick]**. ✔ A strength of the biological explanation for schizophrenia is that there is a lot of evidence coming both from case studies and from animal studies. The findings from different studies support one another **[needs more of an explanation]**. A weakness of the biological explanation is that animals are not the same as humans in their brain structure and functioning, even though they are similar. Humans use the prefrontal lobe area of the brain for problem solving and impulse control more than animals do, for example, though neurotransmitters do seem to work in the same way in humans and animals. ✔ A strength of the idea of social causes for schizophrenia is that there are more people with schizophrenia in inner city areas and there is evidence for social support being important **[needs more such as the evidence]**. A weakness is that people showing behaviour related to schizophrenia might drift into inner city and poorer areas because of their lack of functioning in society that comes from the disorder.

ⓔ **3/6 marks awarded.** The two AO1 marks are given as there is just about enough knowledge and understanding of the two explanations to earn the 2 marks. The strength for the biological explanation is okay as far as it goes, but more evidence is needed to be sure there is an 'explanation' of the strength rather than just a brief statement. The weakness does have extra information, which means the tick is given (but even more detail would be good). The strength for social causes for schizophrenia needs more evidence, such as Brown (2010) suggesting that people with less social capital, in terms of being connected to others and having support, were more likely to be diagnosed with psychosis than those with more social capital. The weakness of the 'social' explanation also needs a bit more detail, such as perhaps more detail about the possible lack of functioning such as not being able to hold down a job or take care of themselves. This answer does focus on the question, but the way it is written is more like a description of the two explanations and a description of the strength and weakness of each. 'Explain' needs a point and then justification of the point, which was done more for the weakness of the biological explanation. This answer shows how important it is not just to know the information (which is good here) but to explain your points fully.

Gender issues in psychological research

(1) Describe gender issues in one area of psychology that you have studied.　　　　(4 marks)

ⓔ There are 4 points-based AO1 marks. This question illustrates the sort of question that might arise, but in issues and debates you would expect levels marked questions. This question is to show how you need to be able to use different areas in the course to focus on the different issues and debates. This question simply asks for a description of gender issues in one area you have studied, so you do not need to discuss or evaluate. **Note:** you could find gender issues in a few areas in your course and describe them, or you could change the question to look at culture, and/or you could use the injunction 'evaluate' and bring in 'two areas' to make it into a 20-mark essay question.

> **Student answer**
>
> One area in psychology that brings in gender issues is obedience. Milgram in his main study in 1963 used just men and found a 65% level of obedience. However, in his variations, which he published in 1974, he repeated the study using female participants and found the same level of obedience. ✔ Kilham and Mann found some gender differences in that there was 40% obedience in males when 'giving' the shocks and 16% in females. Also when participants told other people to give the shocks 68% of male participants obeyed and 40% of female participants did so. ✔ Blass (2012) reviewed the idea of gender differences in obedience and though in 12 studies in different cultures there were two that did find gender differences, including Kilham and Mann, there were ten that did not, so Blass concluded that obedience in general did not show gender differences. ✔ Burger (2009) replicated Milgram's work using both male and female participants and found no difference in gender when measuring obedience. Burger replicated Milgram's findings about obedience, even in 2009, and his finding about gender showed similarity to Milgram as did his overall findings. ✔

ⓔ **4/4 marks awarded.** This answer clearly describes four points that focus on the question and so gets full marks. The information about Burger is not so well detailed but just about enough is added for the mark. The other three points are clear and detailed. For every point in your exams you should use clear and effective communication and add detail as is done here. This is the case throughout your course and particularly in Section C of Paper 3, as this is the synoptic element and end of your course, where you are expected to give detail and depth.

Role of nature and nurture in psychology

(1) Using two examples, explain what is known as the 'nature-nurture debate' in psychology.   (4 marks)

ⓔ There are 4 points-based AO1 marks. This question illustrates the sort of question that might arise, but in issues and debates you would expect levels marked questions. For this question you need to use two examples from what you have covered to show what the nature-nurture debate is. The injunction is 'explain' so make your point using the example and then justify your answer (for both examples). **Note:** you could use different examples, or change the injunction to 'evaluate' to make a 20-mark question.

Student answer

Twin studies are a good way to explain the nature-nurture debate in psychology because they are a way of looking at the effects of genes on behaviour and characteristics, which is showing what characteristics and behaviour might come from someone's nature. Brendgen et al. (2005) is a twin study that shows that social aggression might come from nurture, which means from environmental experiences, and physical aggression is more down to nature. The evidence they give is that MZ twins 'match' more for physical aggression than they do for social aggression. The nature-nurture debate is whether a characteristic or behaviour like aggression is down to someone's nature or nurture, or what proportion of each. ✔✔ Another example to help to explain the nature-nurture debate is obedience. Studies such as those done by Milgram (1963) suggest that obedience comes from the situation and studies in different cultures all tend to find high obedience in similar situations, which is taken to mean obedience is from the environment, from nurture and learning. However, there is a suggestion that obedience might link to personality, such as authoritarian personality, which gives an element of nature, but largely nurture is thought to give obedience. ✔✔

ⓔ **4/4 marks awarded.** Both examples are enough for the two ticks as the point is made and then there is elaboration and a link to nature-nurture in each case. The first example is more detailed than the second, which could have included some evidence relating to authoritarian personality and obedience, but there is just about enough for 4 marks. There are clear links to the question and the debate is clear from the answer.

Use of psychological knowledge in society

(1) Using two key questions for society from different areas of your course, assess the extent to which psychological knowledge can be said to be useful for society.

(20 marks)

@ There are 20 levels-based marks: 8 AO1 marks and 12 AO3 marks. This question about issues and debates is synoptic in that you need to draw on different material from your course. In your course you looked at a key question for society in each of the topic areas and you need to use two of those key questions here. 'Areas' of your course should be taken to mean 'topics', for example, social psychology is one 'area' and cognitive psychology is another 'area'. Remember to move beyond describing the key questions and focus on assessing the usefulness of psychology in explaining the key question. It is also helpful to offer some ideas about how psychology is not so useful, to help with the assessment and judgement aspect of the question. 'Assess' requires you to come to a conclusion and judgement, in this case about how far psychological knowledge is useful for society. **Note:** you could use 'assess to what extent' referring to other issues and debates, or you use different key questions, to change the question.

Student answer

A key question for society is how to prevent prejudice and psychological theories are helpful in making suggestions about how to do this. For example, social identity theory suggests that prejudice comes from in-group favouritism and out-group hostility — the hostility leading to discrimination following prejudiced attitudes. **[AO1]** Football team supporters, the in-group, would see the supporters of another team as the out-group and hostility towards them would follow, for example, because by showing in-group favouritism the in-group members are enhancing their own self-esteem. **[AO1]**

The usefulness of this understanding of prejudice is that a way of reducing prejudice can follow. If an in-group is enlarged to encompass an out-group so that one larger group is formed, this can reduce prejudice. This can happen in cases of war, where people with opposing views, living in one country, might come together to protect their country. Using the football team supporters example, supporters from two teams who might normally show hostility towards one another might come together to support the country's team, made up of players from both teams.

Preventing prejudice is useful for society in an economic sense because it is expensive to police rioting and unrest, for example, and from the point of view of an individual it is unfair and unpleasant to be discriminated against.

Realistic conflict theory is a different theory from social identity theory. Realistic conflict theory suggests people are prejudiced when in competition over resources, as Sherif showed in his study in a summer camp where one group of boys became hostile towards another group of boys when they competed. **[AO1]** Sherif and his colleagues went on to show that when the boys had to work together towards superordinate goals, goals that could not be achieved without the two groups working together, hostility was reduced. [AO1] This is useful for society as when there is competition over resources it can be seen that prejudice will arise and focusing on superordinate goals (such as improving a society's economic position) can help to reduce prejudice.

One difficulty with relying on evidence for these two theories is that it tends to be experimental evidence. Sherif et al. used a field experiment although they did use some other research methods such as observation, and Tajfel, giving evidence for social identity theory, used laboratory experiments. [AO1] Experimental evidence tends to be reliable but can lack validity because of unreal situations being used. Sherif et al. did try to run a 'normal' summer camp but there was manipulation so validity might be in doubt, and Tajfel used artificially put together groups.

Another key question for society is how effective drug therapy is for treating drug addiction. This is an important question because there is a cost to treating drug addiction in terms of economics as well as a cost to the individual and families. Work hours may be lost because of drug addiction, for example, and families can break up. Also if a drug therapy does not work then it is not worth funding, so the effectiveness of drug therapy is important for society.

Public Health England publishes facts and figures. The number of opiate users in England in the years 2013 to 2014 was 293,879 and the number of adults successfully using drug therapy to become free of drug-taking was 29,150. The number of adults receiving treatment for alcohol in England was 114,920. These are high figures, helping to show the importance of this key question for society.

Buprenorphine acts as an opioid and so produces euphoria as do other opioids, but it acts differently from methadone. [AO1] At low doses, it can be taken without the withdrawal symptoms which makes it more effective. The drug is safer and will not move the person into addiction or lead to overdose. The drug has not led to breathing problems and has not shown cognitive or movement problems. [AO1] However, buprenorphine can be abused as a drug, which is a disadvantage with regard to this being a substitute for heroin, but adding naxolone, as happens in Suboxone (a brand name), reduces the likelihood of addiction to buprenorphine.

Knowing about the way heroin functions in the brain, at the opioid receptors, helps to develop drug therapy, which can help someone to come off heroin. The action of buprenorphine is known about, including it being addictive but giving fewer side effects, and this level of detail can help society when it comes to therapy for drug addiction. A downside is that this is still drug-taking, and there are side effects, as well as drugs being addictive. Li et al. (2013) showed that cues for heroin are linked to activation and connections between certain brain areas, such as the limbic system and the prefrontal cortex, and this suggests that cues themselves affect brain functioning. [AO1] Therefore, even drug therapy involving using a substitute like buprenorphine or methadone to help with withdrawal symptoms and addiction might not be enough if the conditioned cues around the addict are not addressed. This is a downside of drug therapy.

In conclusion, it has been shown that there are advantages of knowing how to reduce prejudice and both social identity theory and realistic conflict theory help with suggestions. However, much evidence comes from experiments, which can mean the results of studies are not valid, which would affect how useful the findings were for society. Similarly, it has been shown that drug therapy has been shown to be effective, such as buprenorphine, which is thought to have fewer side effects than methadone. However, such drugs can themselves be addictive, which is not useful and also if there are other factors affecting addiction, such as cues in the environment triggering the drug-related behaviour, then drug therapy might not be sufficient to 'solve' the problem of drug addiction.

ⓔ **13–16/20 marks awarded.** Page 174 of the sample assessment materials gives a levels mark scheme that you can use for this question. First, consider the AO1 in this question, which is the knowledge and understanding. The AO1 points have been noted here (in brackets), and you can see there are quite a few. In the time available to write this answer, there is a reasonable amount of AO1, but it is not very thorough so would not reach the top level. Sherif, Tajfel and Li et al. are used. It would be good to see a few more studies as evidence. However, mention of buprenorphine and methadone gives some depth, as does consideration of superordinate goals and how being part of an in-group can help self-esteem.

The rest of the marks are for AO3. Two key questions are used, from two different areas, and there is some evaluation and assessment, including a conclusion, so the question is answered. There is a good structure to the answer, with each key question being given a few paragraphs and then the conclusion is separate at the end. There is quite a bit of argument about how useful psychological understanding is for society, using these two key questions as examples. The way psychology uses experimental evidence leading to lack of validity in findings of studies is considered, which is useful assessment. Also there is a discussion of the effectiveness of drug therapy, such as there still being withdrawal symptoms.

The conclusion summarises the main points made, which is required. Like the AO1, the AO3 is good and the focus on the question is good. If studies had been used a bit more as evidence, such as evidence for drug therapy being effective (or not), that would add to both the AO1 and AO3 and lift the answer to the top level instead of Level 4.

Issues related to socially sensitive research

(1) Explain what is meant by socially sensitive research, giving two examples from your course.

(3 marks)

ⓔ There are 3 points-based AO1 marks. This question illustrates the sort of question that might arise, but in issues and debates you would expect levels marked questions. This question is to show how you need to be able to use different examples in the course to focus on the different issues and debates. This question simply asks for definition of socially sensitive research and two examples of such research so you do not need to discuss or evaluate. **Note:** you could find other examples, or give a definition of a different issue/debate, and/or you could use the injunction 'evaluate' socially sensitive research using at least two examples from your course, then you have a 20-mark essay, to change the question.

Student answer

Socially sensitive research refers to ethical and moral issues about research being undertaken in specific areas. Culturally some areas are 'sensitive' which means there are ethical and moral issues related to gathering data in relation to wider society. Research can affect cultural groups in a society, for example, depending on the findings, and such research would be 'socially sensitive'. ✔ One example is Raine et al. (1997) who found using PET scanning that people pleading not guilty by reason of insanity to violent crime had brain differences. Social implications are that they are not, therefore, responsible for their crime, or that scanning can be done to show who is likely to carry out violent crime and they can be 'punished' beforehand by being watched and so on. ✔ Another example is Watson and Rayner (1920) who conditioned a small child to fear a pet rat. This in itself might not be socially sensitive, though there are questions about the ethics of the study, but if conditioning is shown to work, a society can use the principles to condition people to behave as society wants, impinging on an individual's free will. This might help some in a society, but might not help others in the society. ✔

ⓔ **3/3 marks awarded.** Socially sensitive research as an idea is defined and there is enough information for 1 mark to be given. Then there are two examples that are not only briefly explained but also linked to the idea of society being affected by the findings of the research, so 2 more marks are given, one for each example.

Research methods

1 (a) primary; (b) secondary; (c) secondary
2 Qualitative: Milgram (1963) noted the reaction of his participants; Sherif et al. (1954/1961) noted name calling and how the groups reacted to one another. Quantitative: Baddeley (1966b) noted words on a list that were remembered; Sebastián and Hernández-Gill noted digit span of participants.
3 (a) Milgram (1963) advertised for his participants and they volunteered, thus selecting themselves. (b) Watson and Rayner (1920) needed a suitable aged child with a suitable temperament and they found one in the hospital, so this was an opportunity sample.
4 (a) One group of participants could learn and recall the categorised list and one would have the randomised list, to get an independent groups design. (b) On one day a group of participants could learn the categorised list and recall it and then the same participants a few weeks later could learn and recall the randomised list. This is repeated measures. (c) Instead of independent groups the researchers could use different people for the categorised and randomised list, but match the people on gender, age, IQ, and memory ability (perhaps tested beforehand by using another list). This would be a matched pairs design.
5 The IV is whether the list of 20 words has the words in categories or not. The operationalisation is having a list of 20 words separated into categories or randomised, it is not just 'categorisation of words'. The DV is how many words are correctly recalled in any order (free recall) out of the list of 20 words, it is not just 'recall'.
6 (a) A possible closed question (ranked) is: 'Rate this statement according to how much you agree with it using the scale "5 for strongly agree" through to "1 for strongly disagree": "I prefer to work with people of my own racial group."' (b) A possible open question is: 'What is your attitude towards people of other racial groups to your own?'
7 Social desirability means someone answers in a way that is socially acceptable rather than giving their own attitudes or ideas. This means their own opinions are not represented in the data, so the data lack validity — the data do not represent the real-life opinions of that person.
8 Unstructured interviewing allows the respondent to lead the interview in that they can choose what information to give and where to explore issues and where not to. This means the data are more valid than structured interviewing, where there is a set list of questions or than semi-structured interviewing where there are questions as a guide even though there can be some exploration.

9 In an experiment the IV is manipulated and the DV measured so these are important variables. All other variables are extraneous variables such as light and sound in the situation or the health or ability of participants. Extraneous variables must all be controlled. If they are not controlled they can become confounding variables, which means they have helped to produce the results.
10 A covert observation means participants' behaviour is not affected by them knowing they are being watched, though the down side is that ethically it is not as sound as an overt observation. A non-participant observation has the strength of the observer having the time and opportunity to record carefully and not to be biased by knowledge of the situation, so a non-participant covert observation is likely to get valid data as biases are minimised.
11 (a) Animals do not have exactly the same brain structure and functioning as humans, for example, there can be more complexity in decision making in humans, which might mean the prefrontal lobe area works differently. This is a limitation in practical terms. (b) Animals can be used to make lesions and to damage brain areas, which cannot be done using humans (which is a strength in ethical terms).
12 Scanning is useful for looking at brain activity to see what a brain area is for, what its function is. Scanning shows areas of activity, such as when using language you can look at a PET scan to see which brain areas are 'for' language. Content analysis is useful to find out about attitudes in the media or images shown on television. Scanning uncovers biological functioning and content analysis uncovers things like environmental influences, so they are very different.
13 Cross-sectional designs gather data from participants at one moment in time so if looking at the effect of age, people in different age groups are studied at one moment. Longitudinal designs follow the same people over time, gathering data, so to see the effect of age, the same people would be tested at different ages.
14 Controls help to avoid bias in data. Biased data are not useful when aiming to draw conclusions about human behaviour or characteristics as data would not be valid. If someone lies in a questionnaire (social desirability) or is affected by the researcher's gender, or if in an experiment the order of conditions affects findings (e.g. the practice effect if one of the conditions is always done second), then data are not useful. Research is often done to affect policy and practice, such as testing the effectiveness of a treatment for schizophrenia. Policy and practice need to be affected by valid data, not biased data.

15 Scores A would show skewed distribution because the mean, median and mode are not similar enough, but Scores B would show normal distribution because the mean, median and mode are very close to one another.

16 A Chi-squared test is the one for test of difference, nominal data, independent group.

17 The null hypothesis is accepted if the result of a test is found not to be significant, as this means that the study did not 'work'.

18 (a) There is no predictive validity. (b) There is no internal validity. (c) There is no ecological validity.

19 The repeated measures design could be a problem as the recall from one room (the office or the library) might affect their recall when they went into the other room. Independent groups would mean a participant either went into an office and recalled in a different room or went into the library and recalled in a different room. If there was a gap between the two tasks (the two rooms) that might work as a repeated measures study but if all done on one day, an independent measures design would be better.

20 An area that has not been well-studied might lend itself to the use of grounded theory and qualitative data, such as experience of something new like an aspect of social media or online friendships.

21 Peer reviewing is where experts in the field scrutinise a piece of work to make sure the results are secure, build on previous understanding, and that there is credibility. If studies were published without such checks, psychological understanding might be compromised.

22 Competence is one of the four ethical principles in the BPS Code of Ethics and Conduct (2009) and it refers to the ability of a researcher or psychologist. (a) They must not work outside of their competence and (b) they must undertake training and learning that ensures they maintain competence relevant to their role.

Review of studies

23 (a) Their design: Baddeley (1966b) asked people to learn 10 words and then to recall them in order. He used an independent groups design for the most part, though used repeated measures when comparing a person's recall at the time of learning with their recall after a break. Raine et al. (1997) used independent groups because they had people pleading not guilty to murder by reason of insanity in one condition, using PET scanning to check brain functioning, and had a control group matched in important ways as the other group. The studies both used independent groups though there were differences in how they did this. (b) Their use of control groups: Baddeley (1966b) had control groups too because some had 10 words with similar meaning and others had words matched in length but not having the same meaning, as a control, and also some had 10 words sounding alike and others had matched works but not sounding alike, so they both used control groups.

24 Watson and Rayner (1920) carried out their study in a hospital but they controlled the environment in the room the study took place in, and the study had artificiality, so it could be called a laboratory experiment. Raine et al. (1997) also did their study in a natural setting where PET scanning took place, and again there were controls, but the 'murderers' were having the PET scan anyway so to an extent it was a field experiment. Baddeley (1996b) used a lab experiment method. *You can see that answering this question is not easy and needs detail.*

25 Raine et al. (1997) reduced 'murder' and aggression to brain functioning and also focused on areas that previous research had found related to aggression, such as the limbic system and pre-frontal lobes and more specific regions. This does not take into account the situation the event took place within or someone's mood at the time, so is reductionist. Rosenhan (1973) asked the pseudo-patients to be themselves, after they had reported hearing 'thud' or 'hollow' in their heads and asked for information about the whole of their stay and treatment in the hospital so the approach is not reductionist in its focus on their whole experiences.

26 Watson and Rayner (1920) showed classical conditioning principles could engender a phobia through association and this learning could be used to pair a fear response to something society wants feared, thus 'brainwashing' someone, which is social control. Sherif et al. (1954/1961) showed that prejudice could be reduced (controlled) by different groups having to work towards superordinate goals and knowing how to reduce prejudice is a form of social control.

27 If someone with hippocampus loss recalls past memories better than more recent ones, this suggests the hippocampus is important in laying down new long-term memories. This is reinforced if someone with semantic dementia (not with hippocampal loss) recalls newer memories better than older ones.

28 A problem is that the neurobiological mechanisms of animals might not be sufficiently similar to those in humans to use the findings to try therapy helping the extinction of a fear response in those wanting to get rid of a drug habit. (Another weakness might be the reductionist vs holism argument, as this study reduces drug addiction and extinction to neurobiological mechanisms.)

Issues and debates

29 Rosenhan (1973) had to make sure his participants understood what they were agreeing to because they had to be admitted into a hospital and it was not clear what would happen. They had to hide medication, for example. He was able to get informed consent because of the nature of the study.

30 Pavlov (1927) in a series of experiments using dogs seemed to focus more on the controls necessary to get his scientific findings than on the dogs and their experiences. For example, they had to be isolated (to avoid any extraneous sense information that would affect the conditioning) and there is not much discussion in his lectures about suitable caging and care.

31 The participants were likely to be admitted and to have to stay in the hospital at least for a while (Rosenhan did not know exactly what would happen). It was more practical for them to talk about themselves truthfully as they then did not have to remember a 'false' identity.

32 Qualitative data are in depth and detailed and so more likely to cover whole aspects of someone's life, which is a holistic approach. There is less likely to be focus on a specific and narrow issue, which would be reductionist.

33 (a) Freud's ideas about aggression being cathartic, which is the psychodynamic approach. (b) Biological aspects of aggression including parts of the brain and their function. (c) Social learning theory accounting for aggression by saying children copy what they observe in role models.

34 A hypothesis makes a statement about what might happen, such as that women negotiating a course laid out with cones in a car will knock down fewer cones than men. Empirical (sense) data have to be gathered because to test the hypothesis someone has to lay out the cones, set up the study and then, importantly, count the number of cones. The number of cones is empirical data. Pavlov measured salivation of dogs in various conditions, and that is an example of empirical data.

35 Bandura, Ross and Ross (1961) looked at children's imitation of aggression and drew conclusions about differences in imitation between boys and girls, as well as looking at whether the person modelling the aggression was male or female.

36 Societies in different cultures and countries tend to differ, but they are all societies to some extent in that people are living together with rules. It might be that a characteristic found in all cultures it has been studied in is one that all societies develop (because of having the same aims perhaps about living together) rather than the characteristic being in human nature. All cultures might 'nurture' in the same way regarding that characteristic.

37 Bandura in his social learning theory used the idea of reinforcement, such as in vicarious reinforcement, and it was Skinner who discussed reinforcement when putting forward the idea of operant conditioning. The two theories are not completely separate and Bandura's theory built on Skinner's understanding and ideas — the two were working at a similar time. Both their ideas are used in therapy today, such as token economy using rewards for good behaviour and cognitive behavioural therapy which involves focusing on how behaviour is learned.

38 In social psychology the use of social identity theory to understand and control rioting is an example of psychology being used as social control.

39 Psychology is the study of mind and behaviour and there is an underlying focus on areas that will help people. Clinical psychology focuses on mental health as well as mental disorders. Individuals with mental disorders are helped if there is an explanation for their symptoms and issues, and also if explanations lead to treatments that can improve their lives. Society is helped by explanations for mental disorders because treatments can follow, people can then be productive in the work place and perhaps their care then costs less as well so there are economic as well as personal benefits.

40 The study of prejudice and cultural issues relating to prejudice can be sensitive. For example, Guimond et al. (2013) looked at the pro-diversity policy of different countries — if the policy is multicultural it shows that such a society has less prejudice than one where the policy is assimilation. This is a socially sensitive area of research because government policy is seen to affect possible unrest in the society and discrimination and difficulties for individuals.

■ Glossary

This section contains definitions of the key terms that you need to know for the topics in this book: methods, review of studies, and issues and debates. They are subdivided into each approach. Note that methods involves a lot more terms than review of studies and issues and debates so the sections are not even.

Methods

Abstract this is the first part of a report in psychology after the title. It is a summary of the whole study. It helps to filter information so that someone can see at a glance what the study was about and what was found.

Adoption studies studies where children who are adopted are looked at, mainly because their environment will not be the same as for their biological family and yet they will share their genes with their biological family. So it can be seen if a characteristic is attributable to nature or nurture.

Aim what the researcher wants to find out. The aim(s) is written at the end of the introduction section of a report of a study.

Alternate/alternative hypothesis the statement of what is expected in a study, e.g. 'young females who have just passed their test are better drivers around a prescribed course than young males who have just passed their test'.

Bar chart a way of displaying data with bars that can be vertical or horizontal and show the proportional difference between scores. An example is displaying two means for data measuring two conditions.

Baseline measure a measure of what would 'normally' be the case so that in an experiment a difference can be tested for. It comes from the control group — the researcher compares the control group with the experimental group to see what difference the experiment has made.

Case study in-depth and detailed examination of one person or a small group.

CAT scanning computerised axial tomography producing a picture of brain tissue and bone using X-ray.

Chi-squared the statistical test used when difference is looked for and an independent design is used, with nominal data.

Closed questions where a respondent is constrained in the answer by being given a forced choice.

Competence one of the four principles of the BPS Code of Ethics and Conduct (2009) relating to researchers and practitioners not going outside their level of competence and maintaining the required level of competence.

Conditions aspects of the IV that are varied, such as gender (male and female) and in-group/out-group.

Confidentiality an ethical principle within the principle of respect. Confidentiality must be maintained by a psychologist though there are times when it cannot be maintained, such as issues around safeguarding. Such issues around confidentiality must be fully explained at the start.

Confounding variables variables that have affected the results and have affected any change in the dependent variable.

Content analysis a method used to analyse written data or data from drawings. Data from documents, tapes, drawings and so on are considered to find instances of key terms, for example.

Control group the group in an experiment that is producing a baseline measure of what would 'normally' happen without the manipulated condition in the experiment, such as the group having their heart rate measured over a period of time but without exercise or intervention.

Controls procedures in a study that make sure that what is done and measured is not affected by external factors such as noise, time of day, temperature, bias from the researcher or anything else. If a study is carefully and well controlled then findings are secure — they are about what they say they are about. Controls are put in place to avoid bias.

Conventional content analysis picking categories out from the data (e.g. looking to see how mental health is mentioned in the media and generating categories) but without theory in mind.

Correlation design a design in which two scores are generated (perhaps from one person), both on a sliding scale. The two sets of scores are then tested to see if there is a relationship between them, such as one score rising as the other falls (this would be a negative correlation).

Counterbalancing alternating the conditions for each participant in an experiment to help to control for order effects in a repeated measures design. If there are two conditions, for example, the first participant does condition one followed by condition two. Then the second participant does condition two followed by condition one and so on.

Covariables in a correlation where two variables are tested to see if when one changes the other changes too, in relation to one another, these are covariables — they covary.

Covert observations where the participants are not aware that they are part of an observation study.

Credibility refers to data that have been gathered using sufficient controls so there is no bias and the data can be added to a body of knowledge. Credibility is also about trusting the researcher's expertise and there not being subjective bias in the results of a study.

Critical values tables tables of figures against which the results of a statistical test are checked for significance. There are special tables for each test.

Cross-cultural data data collected across different cultures to compare them.

Cross-sectional data data collected from different groups at one moment in time — they can be different ages to compare development.

Data results and findings from studies of any sort. Data are what are gathered from a study and can be either qualitative or quantitative.

Debrief an explanation given at the end of a study to a participant, saying what the study was about, what results were expected and how the results will be used. It gives the participant the chance to ask questions and the right to withdraw their data. It is part of the principle of responsibility.

Deception part of the principles of integrity and respect — participants in a study should not be deceived. If deception is necessary it should be minimal and a debrief must tell participants about any deception and check all is well.

Degrees of freedom (df) the number of cells in a table that are free to vary if the column and the row totals are known.

Demand characteristic a feature of a study that gives a clue about what is intended, so that a participant can either try to help the researcher by doing what they think is wanted or be unhelpful. Either way data are not valid so the study is not a good one. It is a form of bias.

Dependent variable (DV) what is being measured — what changes as a result of the manipulation of the independent variable.

Descriptive statistics measures of central tendency, measures of dispersion and graphs — ways of describing data.

Directional hypothesis a hypothesis that predicts the direction of the results, such as whether more or fewer words are recalled. For example, 'recall of letters is greater if letters are grouped (chunked) than if they are not'.

Directive content analysis is where theory drives the categories (e.g. looking for right-wing authoritarian traits).

Discussion this comes after the title, abstract, introduction, method and results sections in a psychology report. The results are briefly reiterated, followed by links to previous research, strengths and weaknesses of the study and ideas for further research.

Dizygotic (DZ) twins non-identical twins, coming from two eggs and only sharing 50% of their genes as would any other sibling. They can be different genders as with any siblings.

Double-blind technique when neither the participant nor the person running the study knows whether a participant is in the placebo or the treatment group, for example. Neither knows which condition a person is in.

Ecological validity the study measures what the hypothesis or research question needs, and if the setting and situation (the 'ecology') is not natural then data are not going to be valid.

Ethics principles of right and wrong with regard to the actions of others or of societies, and issues concerning right and wrong. There are ethical guidelines for the treatment of both human and animal participants of studies. Researchers need to make sure that studies with human participants do not upset anyone and that everyone is treated fairly and with respect.

Event sampling choosing what to observe specifically and then making notes or tallying each time that event happens and not the rest of the time.

Experimental group the group in an experiment which is doing the condition that is of interest, such as being the group that carries out exercise over a period of time to see the effect on their heart rate.

Experimental hypothesis the alternate hypothesis for an experiment (i.e. for any other research method it is called the alternate hypothesis). The experimental hypothesis is the statement of what is expected in an experiment, such as 'more words from a list are recalled if they are learnt in categories than if learnt as a random list'.

Experimental/research design the three designs are repeated measures, independent groups design and matched pairs design.

Experimenter effects features of the researcher that affect the results of a study, such as tone of voice or facial expression. These might lead the participant to react in certain ways.

Extraneous variables things that might affect the results of a study instead of, or as well as, the independent variable, such as noise, heat, light or some characteristic of the participants.

Fatigue effect an order effect that occurs when the first part or condition of a study is done better than a later one because the participant is tired by the time they do the second condition.

Field experiment when controls of an experiment and manipulation of the IV and DV are present but the artificial controlled environment is not, unlike in a laboratory experiment.

Glossary

fMRI scanning uses magnetism to look at oxygen in the blood in the brain to look at brain activity.

Frequency tables show the frequency of each score in a set of data, how many times each score occurs in the data.

Generalisability the sampling works and the target population is represented by the sample used.

Generalising moving from specific results from a sample to say the results are true of others outside the sample.

Grounded theory a way of analysing qualitative data meaning theory is not used to develop the data but comes from the data themselves.

Histogram a graph that shows the frequency of scores in a set of data and the spread of scores, as well as showing the distribution and whether it is skewed or normal.

Hypothesis the statement of what is expected when a test or study is carried out. The alternate or experimental hypothesis says what is expected while the null hypothesis says the opposite — that any results found in a study will not be significant enough to draw conclusions and are likely to be due to chance. Statistical tests look to see if results are significant enough to be unlikely to be due to chance.

Independent groups a research design where different participants are in the different conditions.

Independent variable (IV) what the researcher manipulates in a study — there are usually two conditions (or more) in the study.

Inferential statistics tests to see whether the variables being studied are different or related enough to draw conclusions to that effect. Tests include the Spearman, Mann–Whitney U, and Chi-squared.

Informed consent the agreement of participants to take part in a study on the basis that they know what the study is about, and the principle that they must be given this information before taking part. It is part of the principle of respect.

Integrity one of the four ethical principles in the BPS Code of Ethics and Conduct (2009). It involves a researcher being honest in their work including what they publish and how they handle boundaries with others.

Internal validity this means that any cause-and-effect conclusion drawn from a study is acceptable, in that there is no bias that might affect such a conclusion, and no other 'cause'. As there is not likely to be 'no' bias, it is the degree of internal validity that is important — a study needs as much as possible.

Inter-observer reliability agreement between observers. When more than one observer is used in one study, their observations can be compared. If their observations agree, it can be said that there is inter-observer reliability, because in a way the study was done twice and the results compared. If there is more than

one person rating behaviour that links to inter-rater reliability. If more than one person is doing a content analysis there can be inter-researcher reliability.

Inter-rater reliability when two or more raters independently agree in their scoring or assessment.

Interval/ratio a level of measurement where data are real measurements such as time or temperature. The mean, median and mode are all useful.

Interviewee a person being interviewed.

Interviews gather data by someone asking questions either fully structured with a questionnaire to administer, unstructured where there can be probing or semi-structured.

Introduction this comes after the title and abstract in a psychology report. It presents other research in the area of study, before giving the aims, research question(s) and the hypothesis as appropriate, before going on to the method.

Laboratory experiment there are careful controls over all extraneous variables, an IV is manipulated and a DV measured, so that there are no confounding variables and it can be claimed that the change in the IV caused the change in the DV. The setting is controlled and artificial, hence the term 'laboratory'.

Lesioning a research method used to study the brain and what part is for what purpose. It involves damaging parts of the brain, as opposed to ablation, which means a part is actually removed. Research using lesioning is mostly done on animals or as part of a medical procedure on humans, not just for research purposes.

Levels of measurement ways in which data are scored or measured. There are three main levels of measurement for psychology at A-level: nominal, ordinal and interval/ratio.

Level of significance the level at which the researcher(s) will accept the results as not being due to chance but due to the manipulation in the study. In psychology .05 or better (such as .01) is acceptable, .10 is not acceptable.

Likert-type data a rating scale that uses categories for gathering data. There might be five points on a scale, for example: 'strongly agree', 'agree', 'unsure', 'disagree', 'strongly disagree'.

Longitudinal data are collected from the same people over time and development can be charted.

Mann–Whitney U the statistical test used when difference is looked for, an independent groups design is used, and data are at least ordinal (they can be interval/ratio).

Matched pairs a design where different people are in the different conditions but they are matched so that they are 'as if' the same people.

Mean a measure of central tendency that is calculated by totalling the scores and then dividing by how many scores there are. It is really only useful for data at the interval/ratio level of measurement.

Measures of central tendency the mode, median and mean of a set of scores.

Measures of dispersion measures of how the data are spread around the mean. The range is a measure of dispersion, as is the standard deviation.

Median a measure of central tendency that is worked out by finding the middle score. If there is no middle score the median is midway between the two either side of the middle. For example, out of ten scores the median is between the fifth and sixth score.

Meta-analysis researchers use other studies and merge them to pool data.

Method after the title, abstract and introduction a psychology report presents the method, with sub-headings for design, participants, procedure and apparatus/materials.

Methodology a set of research methods and everything to do with them.

Mode a measure of central tendency that is worked out by finding the most common score. If there is more than one 'most common' score, then all are given. For example, if there are two modal scores, the data set is bi-modal.

Monozygotic (MZ) twins twins that are identical, coming from one fertilised egg and sharing 100% of their genes. They are always the same gender.

N the number of scores in a list, which will tend to be the number of participants.

Naturalistic observation a research method in which the setting is a natural one for the participants and data are gathered only by observation.

Negative correlation a relationship found when two scores are produced, and this is done enough times — it shows that as one score rises the other falls. For example, as age rises speed of driving falls: a 60-year-old will drive more slowly than a 30-year-old.

Neuro imaging involves various techniques to image the workings of and structure of the nervous system. It is the brain that is focused on in clinical psychology. PET, fMRI and CT scanning are all types of neuro imaging.

Nominal a level of measurement that means data are in categories only, with no numbers assigned. If data include whether someone is aggressive or not, they are nominal data. Measures of central tendency are not useful here.

Non-directional hypothesis a hypothesis in which no direction is predicted and the results can be either 'more' or 'less'. For example, 'recall of letters is affected by whether or not letters are grouped (chunked)'.

Non-participant observations where the observer is not part of the situation being observed.

Normal distribution when data are clustered in a 'bell shape' around the mean and the mean, median and mode are more or less the same, then data are normally distributed.

Null hypothesis the statement that any difference or relationship predicted in a study will be due to chance (in other words, there is no relationship or difference as predicted). It is the hypothesis that is tested when using statistical tests.

Objectivity means no interpretation from a researcher and no interference from subjective bias.

Observation a research method used in psychology that can be structured or naturalistic. Naturalistic observations take place in a natural setting for the participant whereas structured observations are set up situations where observation takes place. Observation is the main data gathering method (as opposed to experiments where the effect of the IV is observed but observation is not the main research method because the study is an experiment).

Observed/calculated value the result of a statistical test once carried out. For Spearman, the test result is called ρ (rho). For the Mann–Whitney U, the test result is called U. For the Wilcoxon test the result is T. For the Chi-squared test, the test result is called Chi-squared and is written χ^2. Really the observed value is the term used for the Chi-squared test more than for the others, which are just called rs/rho, T and U respectively.

One- or two-tailed test a test carried out depending on whether the hypothesis being tested is directional or non-directional. A directional hypothesis requires a one-tailed test and a non-directional hypothesis requires a two-tailed test.

One-tailed when a hypothesis is directional (predicts the direction of the difference) then this is 'one-tailed' when checking critical values.

Open-ended (open) questions asking for people's opinions and attitudes in a way that allows them to write or say whatever they like, without being limited in any way.

Operationalisation making the variables of interest measurable and testable. If you wanted to test helpfulness it would be difficult to know where to start, but you could operationalise helpfulness by measuring whether someone asking for directions was shown the way or not.

Opportunity sampling the researcher takes whoever is available to take part in the study. The sample is sometimes called a grab or convenience sample.

Glossary

Order effects effects that occur when the order of conditions in a study (in a repeated measures design) affects the responses of the participant. They include fatigue and practice effects.

Ordinal a level of measurement that means data are ranked so that the smallest score has rank 1 and so on. The mode and median are suitable averages to use.

Outlier a score in a set of data that is a lot different from the rest is outlying and can affect the spread of scores, giving skewed distribution.

Overt observations where the participants know about the observation taking place.

$p \leq .05$ the probability of the results being due to chance is equal to or less than 5%, which is 5 in 100 scores (or fewer) being due to chance (1 in 20).

Participant the person providing the data in a study — the person taking part. The participant used to be called the 'subject' until it was realised that this made them more like an 'object' than an individual with a part in the study.

Participant observations where the person gathering the data has a role in the situation being observed.

Participant variables variables in the participant that should be controlled for such as tiredness or gender.

Peer reviewing means a piece of research is written up as a report and then experts in the field of study scrutinise the work to make sure it is suitable for publication in a journal.

Personal data information about respondents such as their age, gender, occupation, whether they have a driving licence — whatever is of interest to the study.

PET scanning positron emission tomography using a radioactive tracer to look at brain activity to see the functions of different brain structures.

Pilot study a small-scale practice run of a task or survey to find out any problems and put them right before the real thing.

Placebo something pretending to be a substance such as medication when it is actually something else that is harmless, like glucose. It is given so that participants in a study do not know whether or not they are receiving whatever is the subject of the study — or it is given for safety reasons, so that no harm is done.

Positive correlation a relationship found when two scores are produced, and enough participants are tested/scores are gathered — it shows that as one score rises the other rises too. For example, as age rises, the time taken to react to a stimulus rises. A 60-year-old will take longer to react than a 30-year-old, for example.

Practice effect an order effect that occurs when the second part or condition of a study is done better than the first because participants are practised by the time they do the second condition.

Predictive validity this means that a score predicts what it is claiming to predict. If a test for a job application has predictive validity, then a later test of the applicant (how well they are doing the job perhaps) should show that the application test had validity.

Primary data when a researcher gathers their own data directly and does not use data from another study or source.

Qualitative data data looking at quality and detail such as people's attitudes and feelings in the form of words, for example, or pictures.

Quantitative data data in the form of numbers such as percentages or number of words recalled.

Questionnaires ways of gathering data by using items that can be closed or open questions/items.

Randomisation making the order in which the participant does the conditions random, to control for order effects in a repeated measures design. If a study has two conditions, for example, there can be a toss of the coin to see which condition the participant will do first.

Randomised controlled trials (RCTs) where participants are randomly allocated to either a treatment or a waiting list or placebo condition to give representative sampling and to make sure the two groups match except for the independent variable.

Randomising when an experiment requires two groups randomisation of participants into the two groups can help with fairness. There is randomising in a random sample too.

Random sampling when each participant has the same chance of being chosen to be in the sample, which is the best regarding least bias.

Range a measure of dispersion. The range is calculated by taking the lowest score from the highest score. Sometimes you have to take 1 away from that calculation to get the range.

Ranked data data that come from rankings such as rate for attractiveness from 0 to 10.

Reliability data are consistent because a test is somehow done again and the same results are found.

Repeated measures a design where the same participants do all the conditions in a study.

Replicability the extent to which a study is easy to repeat or replicate. A study is replicable if there are careful controls and if there is enough detail about the procedure to do the study again.

Report a study in psychology is written up as a report, which is written using a specific format: title, abstract, introduction, method (design, participants, apparatus, procedure), results, discussion, referencing, any appendices.

Representative sample a sample in which everyone in the target population is represented. For example, if the target population includes all females, then females of every age should be part of the sample, and perhaps females with different educational backgrounds and different jobs.

Researcher bias researcher effects give researcher bias, which means something about the researcher including their interpretation of data or their perception of a situation can give bias and subjectivity affects results.

Researcher effects where some aspect of the researcher(s) affects data such as their age, the way they dress or how they ask questions.

Respect one of the four ethical principles in the BPS Code of Ethics and Conduct (2009). It involves getting informed consent, giving the right to withdraw, and respecting privacy and confidentiality.

Respondent the person giving the answers in a survey — the participant.

Response set getting into the habit of answering in a particular way (such as 'yes') to a set of questions and so continuing in that way regardless. This can happen if a Likert-type scale is used and all the statements are phrased so that 'strongly agree' is in the same direction (such as being prejudiced). Such statements should be mixed so that sometimes a prejudiced person would answer 'strongly disagree'. A particular type of response bias.

Responsibility one of the four ethical principles in the BPS Code of Ethics and Conduct (2009). It involves debriefing participants after a study, and being responsible for their welfare throughout. This principle is about avoiding harm and not 'looking away'.

Results after the title, abstract, introduction and method sections of a psychology report the results are presented (followed by the discussion).

Right to withdraw giving participants throughout a study the right to stop taking part. Part of the principle of respect and also responsibility.

Sampling the way people are chosen to take part in a study. Usually not all the people being studied can be involved, so there has to be a sample.

Scatter diagram a graph used for correlation data where each point on the graph represents one person's/set of scores on two scales. This is the only time a scatter diagram should be used to represent data. A line of best fit can show if there is a correlation or not, prior to carrying out a statistical test.

Schedule in an interview, the list of questions, any instructions, and any other information such as the length of time for the interview.

Secondary data when data are used that were gathered for some other purpose or in another study, so not gathered directly (which means not primary data).

Self-rating giving a rating score about oneself, such as for attractiveness or meanness.

Self-report data are where someone gives information about themselves using a questionnaire or interview.

Semi-structured interview has some set questions though the respondent can still take the lead to an extent and the interviewer can follow the answers up as they can in an unstructured interview.

Sense checking where data in different conditions are looked at carefully to see if they are likely to be significantly different or to show a relationship. This is done by looking at high and low scores, for example, to see what the pattern is.

Single-blind technique used in a study to avoid the expectations of participants affecting results. It means the participants are not aware of which group they are in or what results are expected.

Situational variables variables in the situation such as noise in each condition being different or time of day.

Skewed distribution when there is an outlying score or more than one and the mean, median and mode of a data set are not the same, data are skewed. This affects statistical testing and drawing conclusions.

Social desirability when someone gives an answer they think they should give to fit with social norms — a form of bias.

Spearman's the statistical test when a correlation is being used and data are at least ordinal (they can be interval/ratio).

Standard deviation a measure of dispersion. The standard deviation is worked out by taking all the scores away from the mean average to see how far the scores fluctuate around the mean. Whether they fluctuate or not can show how far they are spread around the mean average, which helps when interpreting the data.

Standardisation making sure that things are the same, such as questions in a structured interview being asked in exactly the same way with standardised wording. This means the interviewer cannot stray from the wording.

Standardised instructions written sets of instructions to the participants in a study so that all participants get the same information and are not biased by being told something different.

Stratified sampling a method of sampling by which the target population is divided into required groups or strata, and corresponding proportions of people from these groups are picked out for the sample.

Glossary

Strength of a correlation a correlation that is close to perfect (+1 for a positive correlation and −1 for a negative correlation) is a strong one.

Structured interview has all the questions set out and all respondents are asked the same questions in the same format.

Structured observation a study in which data are collected by observing and there is no manipulation of the independent variable, but the situation is structured (set up).

Subjectivity a type of bias when a researcher chooses what data to include as results and there is interpretation in the analysis perhaps.

Summative content analysis searching for key words and then counting them (or references to an issue), before interpreting the data.

Tallying making a mark when a relevant behaviour is observed — the marks can then be counted to give quantitative data.

Target population all the people the results will be applied to when the study is done.

Thematic analysis a way of analysing qualitative data where categories can come from theory or theory can come from the analysis. It means grouping such data somehow.

Time-sampling making a tally mark in an observation every minute or at some other specified time slot. This means a better picture is given of what happens during the observation than recording only changes of activity, for example, because the time during which one activity is carried out is recorded.

Transcript a complete typing up of the data in full, ready for analysis. It applies to qualitative data.

Treatment group the participants getting the treatment part of the independent variable.

Triangulation using more than one method to come up with data that can then be compared to look for validity (how 'real life' they are) and reliability (how far the same data were collected using the different methods).

Twin studies comparisons of MZ and DZ twins on certain characteristics to see if there are differences between how frequently the MZ twins and how frequently the DZ twins share the characteristic. If there are quite strong differences then that characteristic is said to have a genetic basis, at least to an extent.

Two-tailed when a hypothesis is non-directional (does not predict the direct of the difference) then this is 'two-tailed' when checking critical values.

Type I error when someone over optimistically chooses an 'easier' level of significance (e.g. $p<.05$) and it is subsequently found that results (of other studies) show there is no difference so when claiming a difference a Type I error was made.

Type II error when someone chooses a tough level of significance (e.g. $p<.001$) and says 'there is no difference' when subsequently a difference is found at a lower level of significance (using other studies).

Universality refers to characteristics that are found in different cultures using similar methods. This suggests such characteristics are in our human nature and not given by nurture.

Unstructured interview when there is a very general schedule to follow but the interviewer can go with the interviewee's thoughts and direction.

Validity data are about real life and what is said to be measured is what is being measured.

Variables whatever influences are likely to affect the experiment, including what is being tested, what is being measured, and anything else likely to affect the results. They include confounding variables, extraneous variables, the independent variable and the dependent variable. There are also situational variables and participant variables.

Volunteer sampling a method of sampling by which people are asked to volunteer for the study either personally or via an advertisement. They self-select themselves by volunteering.

Wilcoxon signed rank the statistical test used when difference is looked for, a repeated measures or matched pairs design is used, and data are at least ordinal (they can be interval/ratio).

Review of studies

Synoptic skills of drawing on different areas and ideas to show an understanding and an overview of something.

Issues and debates

Culture in psychology culture is a variable that can be considered, such as whether multicultural societies have different prejudices than those using an assimilation approach or whether culture affects levels of obedience.

Empiricism this is the idea that knowledge comes only from sense data. Empirical data are data collected by sight, sound, taste, smell and touch — through our senses. Science uses empirical data to test hypotheses that are derived from theories.

Falsification this means looking at a claim (hypothesis) to see if it can be shown not to be the case. The idea is that, for example, we can find helpful females many times but we cannot say all females are helpful. When we find one unhelpful female we can show the opposite is the case (not all females are helpful) — we can falsify but not prove.

Gender in psychology gender is a variable that can be considered in studies, such as whether there are gender differences in obedience.

Holistic approach the idea that to find out about something, the whole must be studied, not the parts. For example, you can study a person's levels of aggression by scanning and seeing activity in the limbic system (reductionist approach), but real-life aggression is more complex: it has a trigger, a type (e.g. physical or verbal) and a background. The opposite of a holistic approach could be said to be a reductionist approach.

Nature–nurture debate the question of how far a characteristic comes from our nature (what we are born with, which is down to our genes) and how far it comes from our nurture (what we experience from our environment as we develop, which is down to our upbringing).

Reductionism this means the way science looks at parts of a whole, in order to use controls and study something systematically. This focus can mean reducing behaviour

to something not 'real' and not 'whole'. Science needs to draw cause-and-effect conclusions and must often reduce what is to be studied to something manageable.

Science building a body of knowledge in such a way that others can rely on the knowledge. This involves objectivity, measurable concepts (so that the tests can be done again), careful controls and the generating of hypotheses from previous theory (so that one piece of evidence can link to another one to build the knowledge).

Social control refers to people being regulated by systems in a society that can affect their thoughts, feelings and behaviour.

Socially sensitive research research where findings affect society in a possibly negative and ethical and moral way.

Theory an idea about why an event happens, usually based on previous theories and research.

Universals/universality characteristics that are found in all cultures and, therefore, thought to be down to human nature and not to nurture.

Index

Index